Shakespeare, Moses and Joe Papp
by Ernest Joselovitz

CAST OF CHARACTERS

Robert Moses, at age 70
Jesse Seligman, a young man, his new secretary

Joseph Papp, at age 37
Jacob Rose, his colleague and friend
Peggy, his wife

Robert Wagner, New York City's Mayor

The Narrator, who also takes on the roles of the lawyer Silverstein, the lawyer Levenson, and the lawyer Schwartz: all of whom wear dark suits, carry expensive briefcases, and whose names are seldom seen in newspapers.

and various voices

TIME
The end of 1958 to August 1959.

INTRODUCTION

Joe Papp has roots in the Jewish culture of Eastern Europe; Robert Moses carries with him the money, class and proud heritage of the German Jew (who were here first). This is a clash between these two men defining two worlds: Robert Moses' world is of a spacial abundance, a facade of orderliness, a world of plaques and folders, a large solid desk, a model of the Verrazano Narrows Bridge. Joseph Papp's world seems at first a cramped chaotic mess, except just about everything in it denotes one set of activities, one ambition: the telephones, the manual typewriter, the changing model of the JULIUS CAESAR set. The two men occupying these worlds seem very different, too: Moses, always in a formal suit and tie, is cool, quiet, his emotions under a control nurtured and defined by experience and birth; Papp, dressed in old slacks and an open shirt, is wired, quick energy. But a closer look, and as their drama unfolds, reveal similarities: a vision not only for themselves but everybody else, and a single-minded driving ambition, carrying in its wake large egos.

This is history as myth. There are significant visual images - a wall of plaques, a model of the then-proposed Verazzano Narrows Bridge, a theatre set model - but the central focus is on the larger-than-life individuals. If it's not noted, I don't "see" it. I have tried, in the writing, to encourage a continuous flow, avoiding stagehands in blue light.

Thanks to: Lloyd Rose, my dramaturg. Lou Jacob, director. Jim Nicola, for the interview. Harold Black, for the Yiddish. Bob Griffin, for the financial legal expertise. Developed with The Playwrights Forum, New York Theatre Workshop, and Round House Theatre.

Shakespeare, Moses and Joe Papp
© Ernest Joselovitz
Trade Edition, 2015
ISBN 978-1-63092-074-6

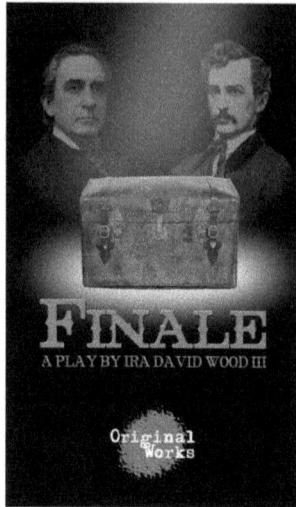

FINALE
A PLAY BY IRA DAVID WOOD III

Original Works

Finale by Ira David Wood III

Synopsis: A haunting tale of family, history, regrets and shame. The Booth family was America's greatest acting clan. Generations of Booth sons tread the boards of American stages garnering great acclaim and riches until the youngest and arguably most famous of them all, John Wilkes, turned the country upside down. Eight years after the assassination of President Lincoln, Edwin Booth returns to his family's theatre in New York to sort through his younger brother's storage trunk which the government has recently returned. Ghostly memories of his father and brother appear to him as he struggles to rectify issues that have plagued his family name since that fateful night at Ford's Theater.

Cast Size: 5 Males, 3 Females

SHAKESPEARE, MOSES, AND JOE PAPP

Robert Moses sits at his desk.

NARRATOR: Robert Moses.

The young man, Jesse Seligman, dressed with the same immaculate easy innate grace as his new boss and old family patriarch, walks in with a set of manila folders.

He stops to gaze at the wall of plaques and citations.

SELIGMAN: Uncle? There's a missing plaque.

MOSES: The Lifetime Achievement Award from the American Society of Civil Engineers.

SELIGMAN: Oh. Great. When did you get that?

MOSES: I haven't yet.

SELIGMAN: Oh.

MOSES: But I will. *(Moses is already looking through his first folder of the day.)* I will.

NARRATOR: Went to Yale University, Oxford, and Columbia. Entered the Civil Service in 1922. By 1958 Robert Moses was the New York State and City Parks Commissioner, controlled the New York State Public Works Department, New York State Power Authority, New York Bridge and Tunnel Authority. Among other things. Robert Moses built every bridge and tunnel and highway in the state and city of New York, every single public house or building, for thirty-five years. By 1958, Robert Moses had built over six hundred parks in New York City alone, and had decided every event in every one of those parks.

Cross-fade to:

PAPP: *(entering)* Jake? I quit!

ROSE: You what?

PAPP: CBS! - TV! - junk! it's junk!

ROSE: A full-time job ...

NARRATOR: Joe Papp, aka "Yussel Papirofsky", son of Yetta and Shmuel, a trunk maker who was usually unemployed. Did not attend Yale or Oxford or Columbia. Graduated high school to work as a janitor, a barker on Coney Island, delivered laundry. Among other things. Then he joined the Navy. Which is when he started to put on shows. After the war he joined a sheet metal factory and the Actors Lab, which was mostly Communists, like himself. He wandered through a few marriages and a job as floor manager for CBS.

PAPP: "I turn my back. There is a world elsewhere." Coriolanus, Act 3, scene ...

ROSE: It's a paycheck!

NARRATOR: Not what you'd call a prescription for greatness.

PAPP: Stop! Jake!

ROSE: You have Peggy, the new kid, the alimony payments.

PAPP: I know - I will. I've still got Shakespeare.

NARRATOR: And oh yes, this man passionately loved the plays of Shakespeare. So, in 1953, at a rundown church on Avenue D, Joe Papp and Jake Rose had started the New York Shakespeare Theatre.

ROSE: Oh you do ... A theatre company without a theatre, not even a budget, that charges no admission for a season of

400 year old plays running outdoors for a few summer months? You understand this.

PAPP: There is greatness here, for me, for you, this is it, right here.

ROSE: Well. But. Giving up your day job....

PAPP: You'll do it, mark my words, someday, you'll be out too, out of that ice box job.

ROSE: Oh you think.

PAPP: Think? I know. My bones tell me, my blood tells me . Joe Papp, Jake Rose - can't you see it? touch it? great things. You're here, with me, believe in this, the two of us. Producers!

ROSE: Maybe so, well sure, well yes.

PAPP: Well yes. Jake. The two of us, the North Atlantic, L.A. Actors Lab, New York.

NARRATOR: Unspoken now, the pain and anger too recent: the House Committee, subpoenas and testimony, the two of them, refusal and defiance, and the blacklist.

Between them, a silence.

ROSE: Hey.

PAPP: Hey. "We have set our life upon a cast...!

ROSE: "And we will stand the hazard"!

PAPP: Right.

ROSE: Right. *(Holds out one of the telephones)* Get to work.

Cross-fade to:

MOSES: *(dictating to Seligman)* "Dear Jerry, Thank you for your article of November-the-22nd, 1958. I am pleased to confirm the accuracy of your reporting, I can always count on your sympathy and your thorough knowledge of the subject. The proposed Verrazano Narrows Bridge will provide tens-of-thousands of jobs, benefit millions of motorists every year, a work of art, commerce and convenience.

"Dear Mr. McConaga, Minneapolis Star, article of November-the-22nd. I am pleased to confirm the accuracy"... so forth so on, the same.

"Dear Mr. Bateman, San Francisco Chronicle, article of November the 23rd. I wish to correct your misapprehension of the facts regarding the displacement of residencies necessitated by the proposed Verrazano Narrows Bridge. It was, I'm sure, unintentional. Attached is the correct information. Our legal counsel will be in touch with you about the wording of your printed retraction."

"Dear Isaac, Atlanta Constitution, "Your article of November-the-23rd ...

Moses notices a manila envelope.

MOSES: How did this get here?

SELIGMAN: Today's 9 a.m. delivery, along with .... oh... my God.

Having opened it, Moses pours out (as expected) large- denomination dollar bills ...

MOSES: You did not see this. I did not see this.

SELIGMAN: A bribe, this is a bribe, it's illegal, I'll report it, we have to report it to the proper authorities.

MOSES: I'm the proper authority, Mr. Seligman, over a dozen unions, hundreds of contractors and sub-contractors. So: no name, no return address, you'll mail it from ... Manchester Vermont. It's a donation - with an unsigned cover letter, " in gratitude for ..." and a request for anonymity-send it to Fordham University. That way Fordham University has a new lab. And my hands are clean.

SELIGMAN: But this particular contractor will think you're obligated.

MOSES: ... when I'm not.

SELIGMAN: But they're breaking the law.

MOSES: An anonymous businessman making a generous donation to Fordham University?

SELIGMAN: But if you don't hire them ...

MOSES: They'll think they've succeeded in breaking the law. And that I wield so much power over construction contracts that I got a better offer. *(He holds out his tight fist:)* I've got them by the balls, Mr. Seligman. (He opens his empty hand:) Without a trace of their dirt, a hint of their stink. *(returning to dictating letter:)* "...Isaac," Atlanta Constitution, "...your article of November-the-23rd, I am pleased ...." so forth so on.

Meanwhile:

PAPP: *(on the telephone)* Me? Am I what? This makes a difference in your charitable donation? *(A beat.)* Well yes, I am Jewish. *(A beat.)* Yes. It's Papirofsky. *(A beat.)* Shalom to you.

ROSE: *(to Papp)* Jewish? You? Your mother knows, I know... Does your wife? ...

PAPP: It's New York, it's the theatre: so now I'll be Jewish. For a donation of $500 I'd be a Nepalese Buddhist.

And then ...

SELIGMAN: Temple Emanuel, the High Holidays.

MOSES: Two seats. In the back, you'll insist. Then purchase two seats... *(finds the envelope)* here, at Temple Israel.

SELIGMAN: Which one will you attend?

MOSES: Neither. Yom Kippur. No disrespect, but on what other holiday does a fella pay $50 for a seat and then never get to sit down? This way I'm happy, the rabbis are happy. Any questions, remember, my wife insisted we attend ... whichever, "the other one." *(A beat.)* Next.

As Moses is handed another, thick folder ...

Cross-fade to:

ROSE: *(on telephone)* Department of Corrections? Mr. Fleming? Jake Rose...We are in dire need of some billy clubs. It's a modern JULIUS CAESAR. One? Two? ...

PAPP: *(grabbing Rose's telephone)* Ten!

ROSE: *(grabbing it back)* Three? *(A beat.)* Three. Yes. Thank you.

PAPP: *(On telephones)* Sanitation? This is Papp.

NARRATOR: ... Papp, Joe Papp, who reached Mayor Wagner, wanting not money, "not one cent, just in-kind services, from a few, you know, city agencies."

ROSE: Actually, yes, there is more.

PAPP: Right.

ROSE: Handcuffs.

PAPP: A pick-up truck.

ROSE: Whatever you can spare ...

PAPP: *(grabbing Rose's telephone)* Ten!

ROSE: *(having grabbed back his phone)* Mr. Fleming? Mr. Fleming. *(He's hung up.)*

WAGNER: Sure, well, sure. Shakespeare.

NARRATOR: ... the Mayor thinks,

WAGNER: ...A couple shows on the lawn, how much could that possibly amount to?

Meanwhile, Papp nods, clicks off, dials again.

PAPP: Office of Civil Defense? Papp here.

NARRATOR: "How much could that possibly amount to," he thought.

PAPP: Paint: that army green, a few gallons ... twenty?

ROSE: *(into telephone)* Housing Authority.

PAPP: *(back into telephone)* Department of Public Events?

ROSE: Jake Rose here.

PAPP: Papp.

ROSE: Scaffolding, metal.

PAPP: Two-by-fours.

ROSE: No? *(Beat.)* Nothing? *(Beat.)* Where? *(Writing it out)* Sewer... Services.

Hands slip of paper to Papp.

PAPP: You have two-by-fours - How many? *(Sign from Rose: four.)* Eight. *(A beat)* Six? OK. By tomorrow.

ROSE: City Armory? Jake Rose. He did? Yesterday/ A cannon? You sent us a cannon?

PAPP: Sewer Services? I could use some scaffolding, metal.

ROSE: Well what have you got in the way of knives and pistol?

Cross-fade to:

MOSES: *(Goes to another folder)* What's this? "Papp ..."

SELIGMAN: Shakespeare in Central Park.

MOSES: What now?

SELIGMAN: He can't ask for donations, that was your ruling. Loophole, he found a loophole: that the Welfare Department actually has jurisdiction over the Park's northwest corner at 81st Street.

MOSES: Which is where his actors passed the hat? *(Moses chuckles, shakes his head in admiration. Then.)* Letter, New York Municipal Welfare Department; we'll have to put a stop to this.

SELIGMAN: But, sir ...

Moses goes to the model of the Verrazano Narrows Bridge. He is slowly pulling out a piece of one of the girder's foundations ...

SELIGMAN: The bridge ... Sir? - What you're doing ... it'll collapse ... sir?!

Moses stops.

MOSES: One piece, permit one weak spot, Mr. Seligman, one loophole, and the whole structure collapses.

SELIGMAN: Yes sir.

MOSES: Send the letter.

NARRATOR: That's the start of it, the way we see it now.. Joe Papp and Robert Moses, hero and monster. Now that they're both dead. Now that years have gone by. Events become memories become... what? - fiction. Hindsight becomes foresight, two-and-two adds up to five. One story and another, first- second- third-hand. "Magnetism", "vision", "genius". Well not here. Not this.

Cross-fade to:

ROSE: Welfare Department. The Parks Commissioner, Moses, got to them. No more donations.

PAPP: No.

ROSE: "Undignified" is what he calls it.

PAPP: *(bolts out of his seat:)* What? - "Undignified" - What's he talking about? - People want the opportunity, a token of appreciation, nothing wrong with that.

He slams paper into his typewriter...

ROSE: *(His hand over Papp's)* Stop.

PAPP: It's not his damn corner!

ROSE: Think - Joe? - think. He ... is ... right

Papp stops: an abrupt silence.

PAPP: Jake - what are you saying?

ROSE: That he's right.

PAPP: Right wrong, we need the money.

ROSE: ...Right about us passing the hat - what are we anyway?
  Beggars?

PAPP: Beggars, well no, but ... Jake - what are you saying?

ROSE: Handouts - there's something wrong - about handouts
  from poor people hungry for a little culture.

PAPP: Hardworking people, family people.

ROSE: Struggling students.

PAPP: Old people.

ROSE: Taxpayers.

It's as if a light bulb has gone off!

PAPP: Are you saying ... ?

ROSE: Tax ...

PAPP: ... money.

ROSE: Government money. Our government.

PAPP: Money for the people ...

ROSE: The people's needs ...

PAPP: ...for a little culture.

ROSE: Like Shakespeare.

PAPP: The people's Shakespeare.

ROSE: Educational

PAPP: Recreational.

ROSE: Like schools. Libraries.

PAPP: Like ... parks.

ROSE: From the City Council. The Board of Estimates.

PAPP: The Parks Commission itself!

Papp whirls to his typewriter. His fingers bang away ...

ROSE: Money for theatre.

PAPP: *(typing away)* Free... Shakespear.... in Central Park.

By now, Papp is busily typing ....

NARRATOR: It was for him, at the time, just another letter, "money for theatre", that's it, that's all.

Cross-fade to:

MOSES: Does he understand the full meaning of the term "Parks Commissioner"? Did I miss a letter here? A written request of some sort?

SELIGMAN: He does pledge not to pass the hat.

MOSES: "Undignified?" He says it's undignified?

SELIGMAN: You said that.

MOSES: Should be unnecessary, he says. When I build him a theatre!

SELIGMAN: He's naive. He means well. It's Shakespeare, after all, Shakespeare for the underprivileged.

MOSES: Oh? He's already taken enough lumber from this department to build a house. And now he demands - demands! - a $200,000 theatre facility? All for what? - for six weeks a year?

Cross-fade to:

PAPP: *(as he types)* "Dear Mr. Atkinson. I want you to be the first to know about this summer's extended twelve week season in Central Park. Be there. Challenge us. Lend us the unequaled prestige of the New York Times." *(To Jake Rose)* Type out another one of these to Watts at the Post, Kerr at the Herald-Tribune, Chapman, with "the unequaled prestige of" the Daily News, ...

And back to:

MOSES: Something's up. What he wants is to settle into Central Park, permanently. *(A beat.)* There's an amphitheater at Corlears Hook. On the Lower East Side - he can go back to his kind of people. Sure. An underprivileged neighborhood - still plenty of minorities, poor people, youngsters, all that. Offer him the Park at Corlears Hook, free theatre, lights, sound equipment, make the offer as generous as you want.

SELIGMAN: That's wonderful.

MOSES: Mr. Papp, I predict, won't share your enthusiasm.

SELIGMAN: I don't see why not.

MOSES: You don't. This is not about Shakespeare for the little guy. This is about Central Park, the Upper Westside, raw personal ambition in the guise of public service. I know, I've seen it with my own eyes - Some people, at the beginning, are sincere. But then there is the power, the money, the means becomes the ends, intentions become excuses, and the public words lose their meaning. *(Pointing them out in Papp's letter:)* "Marginal income people" ... "cultural life" ... "community activity". When I first started, it was " the urban masses", "recreational habi-tat". Mark my words. He will reject this offer. And I will have to get rid of him.

Cross-fade to:

PAPP: *(on telephone)* Papp, Joe Papp. *(a beat.)* But I know you. *(A beat.)* No, Mr. Browne, I'm not offering you Othello. It's Brutus. *(A beat)* "As Caesar was valiant, I honor him ..."

VOICE: *(completing it, with British accent)* "...but, as he was ambitious, I slew him."

PAPP: Except not that way. You're American, this is an American production for an American audience. "They do it with a better grace, but you shall do it more natural."

VOICE: It's an All-Black production, right?

PAPP: Your wife will be a freckled redhead, Colleen Dewhurst.

VOICE: A workshop production?

PAPP: Central Park, 20 performances, 100,000 people.

VOICE: You're not paying me for this.

PAPP: Not all that you're worth.

VOICE: Brutus.

PAPP: "Be not afraid of greatness.

VOICE: Brutus.

PAPP: "... Some are born great, some achieve greatness, and some ...

VOICE : .....some have greatness thrust upon'em."

PAPP: The contract's in the mail.

VOICE: Right on.

As Papp hangs up the telephone, the letter from Moses has been handed to him. He reads it ...

ROSE: He's offering the amphitheater, all the lighting and sound equipment we'd need for whatever number of performances.

PAPP: We can't.

ROSE: No?

PAPP: No.

ROSE: Well ...

PAPP: Jake - It's nowhere, no way, it's ... it's ...

ROSE: ... On the river,...

PAPP: ... At the harbor,...

ROSE: ... Surrounded by abandoned warehouses.

PAPP: That's it.

ROSE: It's inaccessible.

PAPP: Has poor ...

ROSE: ... Visual lines.

PAPP: The accoustics are ...

ROSE: ... Unsuitable.

PAPP: Unsuitable.

ROSE: It is something. *(A look from Papp...)* Not Central Park, no, but ...

PAPP: Central Park... We can't leave Central Park.

ROSE: *(That stops him cold.)* Joe - what are you saying?

PAPP: *(slower)* We can't leave Central Park.

ROSE: But we already do. Those bus-and-truck tours.

PAPP: ... Which costs a lot of time and money.

ROSE: It's what we do, I mean, people who would otherwise never ....

PAPP: Central Park is central, a central location. *(No response from Jake ...)* For Harlem.

ROSE: The college students.

PAPP: The Upper Westside.

ROSE: The office workers.

PAPP: The Broadway crowd. The critics.

ROSE: What we're talking about are salesmen, tourists, bank clerks.

PAPP: Sure! Central Park! - See it! - a place for people of all colors, classes to come together, think, feel together, experience the excitement of the world's greatest playwright.

ROSE: That's right.

PAPP: That's it.

ROSE: Central Park.

PAPP: Where we'll stay.

Cross-fade to:

Robert Moses completing his lunch, sitting at a side tray. A white cloth napkin is on his lap. He sips from a crystal glass of water. He slices and forks pitted fresh pear halves on a small white plate. He is talking to Seligman.

MOSES: *(on telephone)* Is there a problem with this bridge? All of a sudden, I don't know what I'm talking about? - I'm too old? - out of touch? No! *(Slams down the phone.)* The Verrazano Narrows Bridge will be the longest suspension bridge in the world, Mr. Seligman, a bridge so long we must make a 1-1/2 inch adjustment for the curvature of the earth: 9,865 feet end to end, clearance above water of 228 feet. These towers - 72 stories high. A bridge of the future, the first bridge designed by computer, a beautiful bridge, safe, economical, and beautiful. Any man's lifetime achievement.

Just as he looks at his watch, a waiter comes in and removes the tray.

MOSES: And I will get this bridge. Despite the Board of Equalization, Corp of Engineers, the governor, mayor - my bridge, my way, the right way.

Moses goes to his desk, opens a folder, hands a letter to Selig-man:

MOSES: Read this.

Joe Papp, munching on his second hot dog and with a paper cup of coffee, glowering over a model of the JULIUS CAESAR set which is plopped down in the midst of the office mess. A pail now catches drippings from a ceiling leak.

MOSES: You've read the letter - what does it say?

SELIGMAN: There seem to be technical problems at Corlears Hook Park ...

MOSES: *(interrupting him)* What does Mr. Papp's letter say?

SELIGMAN: *(conceding)* He insists on Central Park.

MOSES: And you believe his reasons why?

SELIGMAN: Summer night, on the Great Lawn in Central Park, is .... beautiful, sir.

MOSES: You believe his reasons why?

SELIGMAN: *(referring to letter)* Corlear Hook is out of the way, sir.

MOSES: Poor people are out of the way.

SELIGMAN: Sir: it's bare cement, it smells bad, a wind at night comes off the river ...

MOSES: It's quieter there than in Central Park, easier visibility - I built it that way; I know - easier visibility, a larger stage than Central Park.

Seligman shrugs helplessly.

MOSES: So. That's it. That's the kind of person we are deal-
ing with.

*Papp, meanwhile, hovers over the theatre model set (with
miniature plastic figures):*

PAPP: He's an aristocrat, a hero, an honorable man, a devoted
husband, father. Julius Caesar now seems all-powerful -
but is he? -. The risers slightly off-center, that's good ... at
an angle, in order to see underneath ... So, Caesar stands
atop this riser, it seems solid, but we can see that it's not.

Meanwhile ...

MOSES: *(dictating to Seligman:)* "Dear Mr. Papp ..." It's not
me writing this letter, this letter originates from the office
of my assistant in charge of parks, ...

SELIGMAN: Stuart Constable.

MOSES: That's it. "Dear Mr. Papp ..."

Cross-fade to ...

PAPP: A dictator, who needs to be brought down, and the only
way to bring Caesar down is with Brutus, a man devoted to
the social good ... Or is he? He comes from below, from
under here, at the very foundations.

ROSE: If we want Central Park, we'll have to charge a dollar.

PAPP: Won't do it. *(A beat.)* Caesar's fall must be, you know,
brutal, literally, he crashes down, down, *(his fist thumping
the table!)* and he brings the whole damn edifice down with
him. *(Knocking them over:)* This, this, this. My set designer can do it, yes, we can, yes.

ROSE: He can make us do it. "Crowd control," he says here,
"soil erosion..."

PAPP: What? *(Paying some attention now:)* Baseball causes soil erosion and that's free. The band concerts bring crowds, and they're   ...He just does not understand. We charge a dollar, we'll have to pay union wages.

ROSE: I talked to Abe Katz at Equity, who said so and then apologized, which means he won't budge an inch. He did deny absolutely any recent conversation with the Parks Commissioner ...

Spotlight on Moses, talking into telephone:

MOSES: If this Papp needed to charge a fee - I'm speaking hypothetically here, just a dollar - what would be your union's response?

VOICE: A dollar, a dime, the son-of-a-bitch'll pay my actors more than meal money - gifted people, highly skilled craftsmen, being paid less than goddamn ditch diggers.

Blackout there, as ...

PAPP: Which means he's lying.

ROSE: You think.

PAPP: Which means it's Moses's way of getting me out of Central Park.

ROSE: No. Why?

PAPP: Why? - I ask myself, Why? Because I'm an ex-Red? I'm a high school drop-out?

ROSE: He can't object to Shakespeare. A person who would object to Shakespeare is a person who thinks TAMING OF THE SHREW is about animal training. Robert Moses is not that kind of person.

PAPP: *(shaking his head...)* I was a kid on the streets, a hood-lum...

ROSE: I know, I know - "porch stoop, fire escape, whatever, it's HAMLET, passion, fate ..."

PAPP: I remember it like yesterday, fifteen years old, a cold winter day, sitting on the front porch stoop, reading the Arden edition of HAMLET. And I was thrilled; the words lifted me up, past the smell of garbage, the urine, the noise of the el-trains passing overhead. God, the beauty, passion, the power, of words, I was shouting the lines of Shake-speare. It awakened something in my soul: an electric con-nection, like fate. Out there, look - see?

ROSE: Yeh yeh.

PAPP: *(oblivious...)* ...That man, those mothers out shopping, that news vendor, we people are hungry for words, music, spectacle, theatre, theatre, our common ground, food for society's soul.

Jake is shaking his head, but he can't help smiling.
Papp has stopped cold.

PAPP: Damn - Damn - Son-of-a-bitch.

ROSE: Well maybe ... Well he's a Yecke'.

Papp gives him a look of incomprehension.

ROSE: A snooty German Jew.

PAPP: What's that got to do with anything?

ROSE: You're galitzianish, like me, by which I mean a Slavic Jew, which for Moses means lice and vodka and ignorance.

PAPP: *(He's stiff-lipped now)* We'll give him the dollar.

ROSE: What?

PAPP: We'll agree to his one damn dollar admission.

ROSE: Then what? We'll have to pay union wages, we don't have the money, so we don't have a show in Central Park.

PAPP: He won't know that. So he'll demand something else, something more. Then we'll know - it's not the dollar he wants, it's me and you out of Central Park.

ROSE: No. You're talking about Robert Moses: the man is a public icon, a future statue in stone. He's a cultured person. He'll listen to reason. He'll understand.

PAPP: He wants to break us.

ROSE: OK, make believe you're right. So? Then what? *(A beat.)* Joe? - what are you thinking? *(Another, longer beat.)* No. Joe.

Papp stands firm.

Cross-fade to Moses at his desk. He has loosened his tie. Seligman looks at his watch ... It's late.

SELIGMAN: Sir?

MOSES: I will not compromise on this. "Cost overrun", the price of beauty, it's worth whatever the cost. Ammann is right - the engineer? The designer? - the man is an artist. Look at it: the economy of line and proportion, the hidden strength of steel and concrete. A bridge, this bridge, is more than a road across water. It's a monument to man's intellectual capacity, mathematics and money made beautiful.

SELIGMAN: Yes sir.

MOSES: *(handing over the folder)* So: the answer is "no", no compromise, be firm but polite.

One folder now remains on his desk. Moses glares at it:

MOSES: I don't understand it. This ... *(rummaging his brain...)*

SELIGMAN: Papp?

MOSES: It doesn't make sense. Where would he get the money? Actors, stagehands, whatever, all at union wages. He does not have the money. You've called, you've checked, you're certain.

SELIGMAN: Yes sir, I'm certain of it.

Moses rises, shakes his head, tightens his tie, readying to leave.

MOSES: How's your grandfather Seligman?

SELIGMAN: Fully recovered, sir, thank you. He's taking tap-dancing lessons.

This is amusing if not surprising to them both.

MOSES: Tonight is pot roast. My cook does a wonderful pot roast, you'll join me and Mary. *(A beat.)* Tap-dancing ... He's a good man, your grandfather. I wouldn't have this bridge without him and his bank. ... Tap-dancing.

At the door of his office, he stops.

MOSES: A dollar is not much to ask. A person can afford one dollar for a theatre performance. There are costs. This is not unreasonable. *(A beat.)* Tomorrow, first thing, the public housing project, Battery Park. Not every public house needs to be low-income, built, rented, maintained at a fiscal loss. *(A beat.)* He's bluffing. He can pay union wages? -

then he can pay.... for security guards ... "We've reviewed the figures....underestimated the costs" ... After that, find something else - clean-up expenses, whatever it takes. Pays us in advance, until he can't pay anymore. I want him out of that park. Send it through...

SELIGMAN: Constable.

MOSES: Constable.

SELIGMAN: But, sir, are you sure... ?

But Moses has exited.
Seligman is left with this final folder.

Fade-out.

In his office, on the telephone:

PAPP: Mr. Atkinson, sir, I need your help. I have a situation here. It's about Robert Moses, Central Park, you know, the free Shakespeare. The man wants to charge a dollar, two dollars, God knows why. I have only my principles, and my determination. I am without resources: a leaky roof, a typewriter with a sticky "w", and the dream of a destitute kid on the back streets of New York City, with JULIUS CAESAR in his back pocket, a dream I will not give up. Ten words, a paragraph, an article from you...

Cross-fade to: Robert Moses still looks quietly elegant in his robe and slippers. He's at home. He sits in a lush straight-backed chair. He is behind that day's edition of the New York Times. He lifts the delicate china cup of tea at his elbow: it gets midway and stops. A rumble is heard.

MOSES: Seligman!

Spotlight on ...

SELIGMAN: *(on the telephone)* The New York Times, no sir, I haven't, sir, I mean, sir ...

MOSES: *(standing now. On the telephone)* This nobody gets eight inches on the front page of the Metro Section to talk about "A confusing reversal of past policy."

SELIGMAN: Well actually ...

MOSES: "Mr. Moses' arbitrary order..."

SELIGMAN: Oh.

MOSES: "The actions of Mr. Moses are ill-considered."

SELIGMAN: Oh.

MOSES: How did this happen?!

SELIGMAN: Sir, there have also been calls here ...

Suddenly, silence. Moses waits.

SELIGMAN: Hulan Jack himself, from the Board of Estimate, and Councilman Stark.

MOSES: Abe Stark? Stark himself? *(Seligman nods.)* Well there'll be a formal letter, that's his way. Abe's a good man. What is going on here? My name, my reputation ...dragged through the mud, thirty-six years of my life. Invite him, with his wife ... what's-her-name ....Esther, Tavern-On-The-Green, I want them there, Thursday, the Thursday luncheon, he likes poached salmon.

Spotlight on ...

MAYOR WAGNER: *(into a microphone)* Here I am, fellas, ...

NARRATOR: The Mayor of New York.

MAYOR WAGNER: .... Holding hearings for the largest city budget in the world, here I am facing an imminent strike of city hospital employees. We're talking hundreds of millions of dollars, talking sick people dead people, fellas. And you keep asking me about some "Much Ado" in the Park?! I have complete confidence in Commissioner Moses: that's all, that's my answer: the man is the most respected administrator in this city, this state, the whole damn country.

NARRATOR: The actor Ralph Bellamy was known for his stage role as a crippled young Franklin Delano Roosevelt, and was in 1959 the president of Actors' Equity, a largely ceremonial position. Except when he stood in front of ten news reporters, for the first time in anyone's memory alongside the President of the League of New York Theatres, which represents theatre owners. And what they said was ...

SELIGMAN: *(reading it:)* "Joe Papp brings to us the real spirit of Shakespeare, a Shakespeare for everyone. Bless him. 'Crowd control'? - What could Commissioner Moses be thinking? That struggling students, old people, poor families with their children, that these citizens of ours, wanting to enjoy a wonderful performance of the Bard, are an unruly mob?" And? Sir? If you'll look out your front window ...?

MOSES: What are those black kids doing on Long Island?

SELIGMAN: They're carrying a petition, sir, signed by every one of the 4th grade students at some school in Harlem.

MOSES: I'm taking away their Shakespeare - is that right? - A racist, is that what I am now?

SELIGMAN: Sir? - the call I got on this came from CBS Television News.

A camera flash surprises Moses, who backs away from the window. An insistent door chime is heard.

MAYOR WAGNER: *(at another microphone)* I'll be discussing this with Commissioner Moses.

A telephone rings ...

PAPP: *(at a press conference?)* This is not a new idea, gentlemen, that our people, no matter how poor, what their race, young and old, have a right to the riches of culture, the arts, classical theatre.

MOSES: This is the private telephone of Commissioner Robert Moses! Nobody ... Oh, forgive me, I did not realize, ... Mrs. Roosevelt, I ... But ... Yes, but ... He isn't, he doesn't, he uses everyone else's money ... He did - He told you that. He simply took over the space, Mrs. Roosevelt, he ... If you'll allow me to ... explain.

He stops, looks at the phone: she's hung up on him. Meantime:

MAYOR WAGNER: No comment!

SELIGMAN: No comment!

MOSES: No comment!

PAPP: *(waving the "checks" and a couple of $5 bills:)* Five dollars, fifty, five-hundred! From a third-grader, a housewife, a corporation. In our first day! - Donations amounting to $15,000! If that's what we have to do in order to serve the needy people of this city, we will raise $50,000 to pay for Shakespeare in the park.

MOSES: Son-of-a-bitch.

Fade-out until only Papp and, in the background, ROSE remain ...

ROSE: *(tearing up the "checks")* Somebody might've asked to actually see the checks.

PAPP: It's a theatrical device.

ROSE: Right.

PAPP: I'd say "The actual checks are in the mail."

One might notice a second pail catching dripping water from a second leak. Rose has a letter, which he hands to Papp.

ROSE: We're dead. It's over. He's sent these letters everywhere, to everybody.

PAPP: What - Moses? - There's no name on this.

ROSE: No name, postmark - what? Manchester, Vermont - it's him. "Joseph Papp's a Red - took the Fifth ..."

PAPP: Moses - you're sure.

ROSE: He's done it before. I did not think he'd stoop to this. After all, it's just ...

PAPP: It's not just a couple plays by Shakespeare, it's him and me, it's personal, I made it personal, "culture", "society", all that, is personal.

ROSE: The council members will back off, the unions, the newspapers: this is his signal to them. And that'll be that.

Papp is sitting; he mournfully shakes his head at the letter.

PAPP: "Wisdom and goodness to the vile seem vile."

ROSE: We did make the front page of the New York Times.

PAPP: Councilmen have spoken up for me, the Mayor, ... *(shaking his head in wonder:)* It can't be over.

ROSE: *(shrugs, grunts.)* We'll go back to performing in the other parks. We can do that.

PAPP: No. Goddamn. Not me.

ROSE: We still have a place at the Church on Avenue "D" ...

PAPP: Jake, no, my God.

Darkness ...

The blue light of a dream scene.

Robert Moses, in his business suit and masked, is "onstage" as Julius Caesar:

VOICE: This is your big chance! - finally! - to prove yourself!

(VOICE OF) PAPP: But ... I can't ...

VOICE: You can do it, Joe.

(VOICE OF) PAPP: Me?

VOICE: Who else? Lee J. Cobb is blacklisted.

Joe Papp is in his underwear. He is "offstage", scrambling through a paperback text of JULIUS CAESAR.

PAPP: But ... the lines ...

MOSES: "The Ides of March are come."

PAPP: *(grabs a knife-holster)* But where are my pants?

MOSES: "The Ides of March are come."

Papp is shoved onstage.

PAPP: "I kiss thy hand, but not in flattery, Caesar."

MOSES: "In the world; tis furnished well with men, ...

PAPP: "Yet in the number I do know but one
That unassailable holds on his rank,
Unshaked of motion, ...

PAPP/MOSES: "And I am he."

Papp, as Brutus, pulls out his knife, but it's only a handle.

PAPP: This is a nightmare - right?

He finds "Caesar" pulling off his mask to reveal himself as Robert Moses, and pulling out a really big (but obviously cardboard) knife!

MOSES: "Fly not, stand still, be not affrighted!."

PAPP: That's my line! I'm Brutus! *(Being chased over the stage...)* Cut! It's over! Time to wake up!

MOSES: *(stalking him)* "The pound of flesh which I demand of you ...

Stops, waves Moses's knife away, which is easy since it's cardboard:

PAPP: What?!

MOSES: "Is dearly bought, ...

PAPP: Wrong play!

MOSES: "...is mine, and I will have it!"

Papp has stumbled to the side of the stage, picks up the prompt book, only to find it's ...

PAPP: But ... we're doing THE MERCHANT OF VENICE? I haven't read MERCHANT OF VENICE for years ...

MOSES: "Mazel tov, Yossel Papirofsky!"

Moses, over Papp's hunched back, plunges his knife with brutal force, to the amplified sound of awful tearing and a thump.

A moment of total shock then a blood-curdling scream from Papp, as blood gushes over his chest from what seems a dozen wounds. A brief blackout.

(VOICE of) PEGGY: *(faintly at first)* Joe? ... Joe ... Joe ...

The click of a lamp, a single light ... Papp sits up, sweating and disheveled, with his wife, Peggy.

PAPP: What? Where am ... ?

PEGGY: Here, Joe, sweetheart, you're shaking.

PAPP: Damn. Oh damn.

He is shivering. She wraps a blanket around him. He is sobbing, trying to get control of himself by breathing evenly, deeply.

PEGGY: It was a nightmare. It's over.

She embraces him. She begins to cry with him, in sympathy.

PEGGY: It hurts. I know. My God. Every night. Let go - You're tied up in knots - Why can't you let go?

PAPP: Oh God.

PEGGY: Joe. Breathe. Talk. Say... something.

PAPP: I feel ...

PEGGY: What?

He falls to his knees, clutching at his chest.

PEGGY: Joe? Joe?

PAPP: I am... I am ...Dying.

PEGGY: You are not dying.

PAPP: Feel small, stupid, nothing, I'm nothing to those people.

PEGGY: *(quieting him...)* Don't... Don't you let it take hold of you. Open your eyes. Look at me. At me.

PAPP: Not... will not ... let this ... h-happen.

PEGGY: You're here. With me. Damn fool. Love you. Joe? *(She is wiping his forehead, his face ...)* "He calls thee dog before he has a cause,...

PAPP: "... b-before he has a cause,/ But, since I am a dog, beware my fangs."

PEGGY: Up. Get up.

PAPP: Yes.

He's breathing desperately, unevenly, but he rises.

She is already handing him his pants, slipping on his shoes ...

PEGGY: Do something - I think you know you have to do something.

PAPP: I can't. I don't... know... what....

PEGGY: What, well, what, there's always one more person, organization, whatever, newspaper...

PAPP: I'll... I'll go to the office. Telephone ...

PEGGY: Well no, Joe, it's 3 a.m.

PAPP: Write... I'll write ... something, a letter to him, some-
    body, ...

PEGGY: A press release.

PAPP: Press release, that's it, Atkinson.

As he exits...

PEGGY: Jacket?

But he's already gone...

PEGGY: Peggy is tired. Peggy goes back to sleep.

Blackout.

*A while later. The not-very-rhythmic banging of typing. The
office: an overhead light. Papp, who never did button his shirt
or lace his shoes.*

NARRATOR: It could have ended right here. It's easy to miss
    a moment like this. You look back, you see it all as inevi-
    table, the sweep of events. Or figure that Moses and Papp,
    one or the other or both, right here right now, see the whole
    thing full and clear: inspired men, visionary men. That's
    not reality, that's the stuff of legends. Here, now, you're
    seeing one foot put in front of the other, one thought and
    then another, feeling good bad bored, whatever. Does this
    man look "inspired" to you?

Rose drags himself in.

NARRATOR: Or this one?

Seeing Papp, he's surprised... Who sees Rose, and grunts.

Rose rips out the sheet of paper in the typewriter.

ROSE: *(reading it)* "I was a commumist. I never jid this fart."

PAPP: "Fact"! - "I was a communist. I never hid this fact." You know, this is no big secret. Anybody could have known this just reading the papers last year.

ROSE: *(crumples the paper and tosses it.)* It's hopeless.

PAPP: *(retrieves it, un-crumples it, reads)* "I was a communist. I am not ashamed of this."

Papp falls to silence, until finally:

PAPP: I am a political person, an idealist.

ROSE: But?

PAPP: But? *(A beat.)* "I was a communist. I never hid that fact. I am not ashamed of it. *(Typing it:)* "I am an idealist, activist, a political person. But ..." *(Stops; stumped.)* "I was ... not ashamed ... a political ..."

ROSE: But what's it got to do with Shakespeare?

PAPP: That's it.

ROSE/PAPP: *(typing it out.)* What's it got to do with Shakespeare?

PAPP: *(continues to type)* "I'm also Jewish. I'm also a war veteran."

ROSE/PAPP: What's it got to do with Shakespeare?

PAPP: Yes! The moon does not fall out of the sky, the planets do not stop circling the sun, Joe Papp and Jake Rose do not give up this, this, our life's work. *(rehearsing his lines:)* "I was for fifteen years a dedicated rabble-rousing card-carrying communist. So what?" ... No.

ROSE: *(scanning Moses' letter again.)* It won't work. Nothing will work.

PAPP: What he's done here is wrong.

ROSE: I don't see how ... .

PAPP: I can make him put a name to this letter.

ROSE: We have no proof. You can't just accuse ...

PAPP: Sure I can! Angry: "Only a coward ... " No. Shocked: "I can't believe a man of his stature ... Disappointed, that's it, I'll be disappointed. "That a man I've always thought of as a hero, a class act, makes accusations against me, and he doesn't have the decency to sign his name." *(an idea!)* I'll make it a challenge!

He's already grabbed a telephone, and is dialing ...

PAPP: *(rehearsing the lines)* "I'm a war veteran. I'm proud to say. I'm a Jew. Proud to say. I was briefly at one time in my life a communist. What's all that got to do with Shakespeare? Bob Moses would have to answer that question. That's why Bob Moses did not put his name to this letter. I want an answer. I want Bob Moses to put his name on this letter of his." *(Into telephon:)* Atkinson, drama desk.

Fade-out.

SILVERSTEIN: Now the real story begins: "Enter Silverstein"... Could be Harry Silverstein ... or Fred ... *(makes up his mind:)* Sam... call me Sam Silverstein. A lawyer, the lawyer, almost anonymous, almost invisible. A name, a dark suit, an expensive briefcase. A name seldom seen in the newspaper, never under a picture, never in a headline. Time goes by, and people like me are forgotten, we're not even a footnote. It's all Papp, Moses, and Wagner. But then, oh yes, then it was "get me Silverstein", as in "We have here a delicate situation", as in "confidential arrangement". Then it was an important name in the political world of, let's say, the Mayor of New York, or the business world of certain bankers. Or in the world of Robert Moses.

Lights rise on Seligman and, in his home, Robert Moses.

SILVERSTEIN: Jesse.

SELIGMAN: Sam. Mr. Moses can give you five minutes.

SILVERSTEIN: Your grandfather's ...?

SELIGMAN: Tap dancing.

SILVERSTEIN: *(nods.)* Hey.

Seligman leads him into the room. Moses, in his robe, sits in the straight-backed chair, before a portable desk stacked with folders, one of which is open before him. Except he now has a business card in his hand.

SILVERSTEIN: I do apologize for intruding, Mr. Moses. It was necessary. This is important.

MOSES: Mr. ... Silverstein? *(Seligman whispers in Moses's ear ...)* Ah ... those Silversteins.

He motions for Seligman to bring over a chair for the man, who motions his refusal, remains standing.

SILVERSTEIN: This is, you understand, a social visit. *(A nod.)* The public squabble between yourself and Mr. Papp must be ended.

MOSES: Squabble? - Mr. Papp? *(As if trying to remember)* He does what? Theatre, isn't he? In Central Park. Squabble? We don't squabble. We have responsibilities. I am a public ser ...

41

SILVERSTEIN: One Jew accuses another ...

MOSES: YOU HAVE INTERRUPTED ME, MR. SILVERSTEIN!

Dead silence. Moses has stood bolt upright, knocking over the portable desk, the folders flying. Moses slowly calms himself. Seligman straightens the desk, gathers together the spilled folders. Moses sits.

MOSES: ... Public servant, have been a public servant for forty years. I take my responsibilities, which are considerable, I take my responsibilities with the utmost seriousness.

Silverstein takes a long time responding.

SILVERSTEIN: One Jew, a respected leader, ...

MOSES: Jewish? Me? I am one thousand things before I am incidentally "Jewish".

SILVERSTEIN: "Jewish" is the public perception: first for them, foremost for them, a Jew is a Jew. And when one accuses another Jew of being a communist ...

MOSES: Someone sends a letter around ... certain facts about a man's politics, facts about his lack of finances, distributes a factual letter.

Silverstein looks to Seligman, who glances away.

SILVERSTEIN: The letter, as you know, was unsigned. Mr. Papp has declared it was you. (Handing them one after another to him) Advanced copies of tomorrow's newspapers, they all accuse you. Everyone seems to presume ...

Moses is quickly reading one after another of the articles.

MOSES: Trash ... trash ... *(well , not this one, or the next ...)* This is all speculation. Libelous, my lawyer will point out to ... A man like me, in the public spotlight, this sort of thing ... I don't understand. A person, whoever it might be, accuses a bank robber of robbing banks. Is there something wrong with that? This man disrespects the laws of this land. I'm a public servant - he's a communist! If I'm a Jew - he's a communist! *(Calms himself ...)* Papirofsky? A Jew? - Since when? - Changes his name, tells everyone that his mother was English High Church, his father Polish Catholic. Suddenly, two months ago ... *(to Seligman:)* Show him the file, where's that file. A Jew? with more divorces than degrees? What kind of Jew is that?

SILVERSTEIN: With all due respect, Mr. Moses, I was not sent here to argue. This Rosenberg espionage business, the Hollywood Ten, are fresh in the minds of the public. People might get the impression that all Jews are communists. This is no time for us - the survivors - no time for us to fight each other. A thing like this, in this heated atmosphere, is fuel for anti-Semites. It is time for solidarity, for caution. It's time for us to stay out of the public spotlight.

MOSES: Spotlight? - what spotlight? - a few days, a few stories in the paper. What do you think I am? I don't ask for a spotlight. I'm not some elected politician pandering for some votes. I'm not some special interest pawing my way to the public trough. I get things done. I build bridges, buildings, roads and parks. You tell me? I run the men who run New York!

He stops. Silence.

Silverstein shakes his hand:

SILVERSTEIN: Sir.

Moses motions to Seligman, who is there to accompany Silverstein out. Which he does.

SELIGMAN: He's not like this.

SILVERSTEIN: No?

SELIGMAN: It's something, it's this Papp, I don't understand, he's not like this. He is a brilliant man.

SILVERSTEIN: Sensible - I'll settle for sensible. Talk to him.

Mayor Robert Wagner is walking cross-stage. He's carrying folders. He's putting on a clean tie. Keeping up with him, the lawyer ...

WAGNER: Three minutes, Levenson.

NARRATOR AS LEVENSON: The suit, the tie, the expensive briefcase: just another nobody, a Mr. Nothing, call him Levenson. As in "We've got a problem here, Levenson."

WAGNER: We've got a problem here, Levenson.

LEVENSON: This Moses-Papp thing - I got your phone message.

WAGNER: What in hell is going on here? Am I missing something? What I see is, I'm squeezed between a bagel and a hard place, squeezing out votes, votes, Jewish votes, and that's your bailiwick, Mr. Levenson. Jesus H. Christ Commissioner-of-Everything gets annoyed at a gnat on his nose, and slaps it off. And now it turns out the gnat is attached to a bear. If it was a fight over turf, I would weigh on the scale who's got what, push some pull some, and it's over. If two guys are measuring cocks, I can do a deflation, it's over. This is not them. I got a sixth sense that I'm seeing black-and-white, and this is a technicolor movie. Tell me, Mr. Levenson, teach me.

LEVENSON: What you might not understand is that Moses is a member of the old families, mostly German, merchants

44

and bankers, some of them here before the Civil War. Papp's kind of people came over around the turn of the century, mostly Russians, Poles, Slovaks, low-lifes, Litvaks. On one side condescension, the other resentment - sense of superiority, years of inferiority.

WAGNER: Like different clans.

LEVENSON: Not quite.

WAGNER: Northern Irish, Irish Republicans.

LEVENSON: Not quite.

Wagner gives him a threatening look.

LEVENSON: Yankees, Dodgers.

WAGNER: Got it.

He's gone.

Spotlight on:

PAPP: *(on telephone)* My second show, when I get the second show, will be THE MERCHANT OF VENICE, in which a Jew is not only blacklisted for his beliefs by hostile right wing Christians, but is betrayed by his own people, a Jew like himself:
"You take my life
When you do take the means whereby I live."

Blackout.

Moses sits in the straight-backed chair, now with a shawl draped over his shoulders. He's looking older. The portable desk, cluttered with folders, has been put aside.

SELIGMAN: Another call from the Mayor.

Moses does not answer.

MOSES: Cars lined up single-file - out there, in those days - on roads kept unpaved, over pot-holes past locked gates and high walls, private beaches and untouchable forests, whole forests. That was Long Island in the 20's. Owned by, controlled by the richest men in the world - Pratt, Winthrop, deForest, Vanderbilt, Whitney - greedy, narrow-minded, self-serving ... You know, they had a golf course - Timber Point - built it simply to prevent a sale of the land to outsiders - twelve members, a whole golf course - and, and your grandfather was not allowed.

He stops, awaiting a response from Seligman, who actually says:

SELIGMAN: Would you like more tea? Orange juice? Sir? I really do think you should have your temperature taken again.

MOSES: I had my chauffeur drive me over every foot of every one of those roads; I had him row me along every inch of the North Shore, South Shore. All of that, just 25 miles from Queens, Brooklyn, Manhattan, millions of people, a car-ride away from sunshine, greenery, an ocean breeze. Cars, everybody buying cars, with nowhere to go. One night, never forget, poring over the maps, books, must have been 2 a.m. - and there it was! like a dream, a vision! suddenly, I could see the whole thing, I'd found my life's work.

NARRATOR: A bill, hardly noticed, paragraph 59 of the State Conservation Act of 1924, established the Long Island State Conservation Commission. And Robert Moses was appointed its first Commissioner.

MOSES: I saw the two parkways - "park-ways" - wide and smooth, no stoplights, no trucks, roadside trees and flowers, panoramic views along the way - I saw boating on Hampstead Lake. Where there was nothing, rocks, I saw bathing at Jones Beach. I saw a sand dune, for me it was a park on Fire Island.

NARRATOR: You slipped in that new word, "parkway", in order to bypass the counties, which had authority over "roadways". You're remembering that now.

MOSES: I jumped out of my chair, had to walk, do something, whirl 'round in the sheer excitement, the electricity of it, slammed my fist into the wall which woke up Mary, heaven knows what she must have thought ...

NARRATOR: You invoked from an obscure law of 1872 the words "land appropriation", hid it as a footnote, giving you absolute power: the way you put it: "I can take over your front yard without a court order and without a cent, and arrest you for trespassing when you come back for the lawn chairs". You're remembering that now.

MOSES: *(he's nodding his head, smiling at the thought)* I got a freshman Assemblyman to sponsor the bill, one of their own, elected by their own, right under their noses.

NARRATOR: You'd lied to him ...

MOSES: And I waited until the rush and confusion of the final day of the session.

NARRATOR: ... Then you slipped it past the governor, who signed it. And charmed the environmentalists, who supported it. And intimidated the farmers, the fishermen whose land, whose shore, whose lives were to change forever. You're remembering that, how you did that, knowing you had to do those things.

MOSES: I haven't thought about that for years. The power, the size, the absolute rightness of it. Where did it all go? *(A beat.)* This bridge, the Verrazano Bridge, has four cables, each 36 inches in diameter, each a mile long. Will be a beautiful, beautiful bridge. *(A beat.)* Where are the newspapers? I haven't seen the newspapers today.

SELIGMAN: Well, sir, ...

MOSES: They're still bad.

SELIGMAN: The ACLU is demanding your apology for that letter. Jacob Javits made a speech yesterday on the floor of the U.S. Senate. Mayor Wagner has offered a special $20,000 city appropriation, Papp won't take less than $50,000, as a guaranteed line item every year. The B'nai B'rith ...

MOSES: What do you think, Jesse?

SELIGMAN: Me? Sir? I .... wish you'd let me take your temperature ... *(no response)* To have this position, to be this close to a man like you - I can't tell you, how honored ... *(A beat.)* You do have the authority, sir, without question, and there are real costs involved, and one dollar or two is not much to ask, and ...

MOSES: Jesse. I built a golf course that your grandfather could play on. I fed pablum and property loans to your father. I want your honest answer.

SELIGMAN: You are correct about all that. You might even be right about this Mr. Papp's motives. But ...

MOSES: But ...

SELIGMAN: You're against Shakespeare in Central Park, free to everyone.

MOSES: I'm building, right now, public housing for more people than will ever go see his Shakespeare show.

SELIGMAN: *(shaking his head)* Don't you see? - Thirty-five years ago you built parkways - sculptured bridges, landscaped dividers, hillside views - something beautiful for anyone with an automobile. Made possible an accessible beach, free, for the average person.

MOSES: *(a beat.)* Thirty-five years. *(A beat.)* Shakespeare ... Hmmmm... *(he closes his eyes, nodding assent.)* On the Great Lawn ... "And there the antic sits/ Allowing him a breath, a little scene,/Infusing him with self and vain conceit,/Comes at the last and with a little pin/Bores through his castle wall, and ... farewell....king." *(A beat.)* I can't ... I can't let go of this.

SELIGMAN: I know.

MOSES: Why? - why can't I let go?

The telephone rings. Seligman doesn't dare move to answer it.

SELIGMAN: ... The Mayor again.

Moses throws off the shawl from his shoulders and stands:

MOSES: I'm sick I'm tired. *(yelling out for her)* Mary?! *(Back to Seligman)* Only Mary will be allowed to talk to the Press: "Hospital, viral something-or-other, won't be available to anyone." The Boss is out. The Mayor will have to wait.

Blackout.

END OF ACT I

ACT II

Joe Papp is banging away at his typewriter. A telephone is propped between his shoulder and ear. It's Mayor Wagner at the other end: in his limousine, shaving with an electric shaver. He's sipping a whiskey.

PAPP: Mr. Mayor.

WAGNER: This interview, for godsake, I put on the morning news, "Mayor Wagner said this, promised that."

PAPP: I get asked questions, your Honor, I get misquoted.

WAGNER: Joe, this public pressure has to stop. I am on your side, Joe.

PAPP: It's not me. I spend my time on Shakespeare. A cause like this - art, theatre goes deep, to the heart of a people - takes on a life of its own. It's out of my control. I'm as surprised as you are.

WAGNER: Sure you are.

PAPP: I'm sorry to see you caught in the middle of this. Believe me, it's not my intention. *(covering mouthpiece)* WNEW? Make it for ... two-fifteen. *(To Wagner)* If only you and he would meet - he's a reasonable man, you're the Mayor - I'm sure this would be resolved. It's a matter of communication.

WAGNER: He's being hospitalized, what can I do?

PAPP: My heart goes out to him. There comes a time when the workload, the responsibilities, are more than a person can handle. It could be a virus like he claims, it could be something worse, something - god forbid - more long-term. Then what? Meanwhile I have a show to put on: actors to hire, sets to build, lights, P.R. All Moses has to do is stay sick and I'm dead.

Meantime,...

WAGNER: Stop the car.

*... Wagner's limousine has stopped. Levenson enters to sit op-
posite him, immediately opens his briefcase. The trip continues.*

WAGNER: *(still on telephone)* I gave you my word - The
meeting with Mr. Moses is as good as set.

Levenson shakes his head at what he's just heard.

WAGNER: 99%. Don't quote me: this is not a rehearsal of a
play script, to repeat every line, it's a private conversation.
(Covering mouthpiece) What's all this?

LEVENSON: It's a stone wall: Robert Moses. Take two aspi-
rin; beat your head against it.

WAGNER: You announced, made a public announcement,
raised - what? $40,000.

PAPP: I did say that.

WAGNER: Joe. Joe. I'll write you a check - right here right
now - from what's called discretionary funds, the entire
amount needed by Moses. What is it, what could it be? -
(looking to Levenson) twenty ... thirty ... fifty....fifty... one
thousand dollars?! *(That causes him to pause.)* The place
will be yours to use, you'll have money of your own to
spend - that should be enough to get you started. So: announce you're hiring actors, show a watchyacallit set de-
sign. Get the heat off me.

PAPP: Without a commitment to our performance space?
Maybe I can pay the designers, technicians, the actors,
equipment and supplies ... But as you yourself said, your
Honor, what the Shakespeare Theatre needs is a line-item
on the annual budget ...

WAGNER: I said...? I never ... ! Don't you do that, Joe, don't you tell the press that.

Wagner gulps down the rest of his whiskey.

PAPP: Me? It's not me. What would I know about city budgets? I'm quoting Councilman Stark - did he misunderstand you?

WAGNER: Abe Stark won't have the votes to toast a bagel without my support, and he won't have my support if you don't stop squeezing my sweet Irish dumplings as a public entertainment!

Wagner slams down the telephone. Blackout on Papp, as Wagner immediately taps what would be the separating window:

WAGNER: Call Councilman Stark's office, I'll be there at ... four today. And stop off at Zabar's for one pound of their best Nova lox.

As he's tying his tie ...

WAGNER: I am the Mayor of the biggest city in the richest country the world has ever known - tell me, why can't I get a cockamamy civil servant into my office? I pay his salary!

LEVENSON: No, actually, you don't. *(holding up a thick folder)* These are his titles. This one ... is at the discretion of the Mayor's Office, and... this one by the City Council. State governor, legislature, this one is federal... state, one borough, another borough, federal and state ...These are all non-elected, all for different lengths of time, ending on different years: an overlapping maze of jurisdictions.

WAGNER: Damn. Damn. Son-of-a-bitch is hanging me out to dry. *(Grabbing the sheet:)* This one, I've got authority over this one, "Look," I can tell him, "thank you very much, here's your gold-plated pen, don't slam the door on your way out'."

LEVENSON: He'll tell you, "file specific charges of miscon-
duct, hold a formal public hearing, both sides represented
by counsel".

*Mayor Wagner scans the sheet handed him, shakes his head at
Levenson in awe.*

WAGNER: The man sure knows how to write a law.

*Wagner takes another sheet, then another, continuing to shake
his head in wonder as he reads through them.*

LEVENSON: And use it.

WAGNER: There is no other way I can put pressure on him.

LEVENSON: Because he's got independent income.   Holland
Tunnel, Triborough Bridge,   Hudson Parkway ... Tolls
used to end once a bridge, a road, was paid for.   Until
Robert Moses added a few words about "maintenance" and
"at the discretion of ..." Income he uses as collateral, so he
can issue ... his own ... bonds.

Something has definitely gained his rapt attention.

LEVENSON: Bonds... bonds...

While ...

WAGNER: Everybody is under the impression that I was
elected to actually run this city. Sure. I can't get the city
budget past the City Council. I can't get union nurses back
into the hospitals. I can't get the Parks Commissioner to
talk to me, explain how to him free Shakespeare is a communist plot.

LEVENSON: *(his attention still on the folder)* Uh-huh.

WAGNER: Levenson! I won't be run out of office by two Jews fighting over "Hey Nonni Nonni" in Central Park! You've got to get me into that hospital room, give me ten minutes, he can be unconscious for all I care, I'll make something up, I'll get this off page one.

The limousine screeches to a sudden halt.

WAGNER: *(to Levenson)* The morning papers.

As Wagner slips in his suit jacket, brushes his hair, freshens his breath, Levenson exits offstage, returns with a pile of daily newspapers, which he plunks on the Mayor's lap.

WAGNER: We can announce his request to meet with me at the hospital. I'll accept, I'll arrive there. If he says "no" to the deal, it's attributed to his illness. If he goes along, ...

Levenson puts one out from the pile and puts it in Wagner's view.
Wagner stops at mid-sentence, and can only stare at the news article before him.

WAGNER: Damn. Damn. He must have done this last night. No phone call to me, no letter. He doesn't request, no, he announces, not to me but to the New York Post ... Daily News ... The Times... What if I don't have my calendar free at one p.m.? What if I'm not free to meet him at the "Tavern On The Green?"

Spotlight cross-stage on Robert Moses, ensconced at a large table set for lunch; white tablecloth, napkins, china and the pastels of flowers and lush greenery punctuated with sparkling lights. At one corner, a sideboard of handsome, silver-covered serving dishes, utensils.

LEVENSON: I think, your Honor, that you will be.

WAGNER: *(It only takes him a moment to realize...)* Right.

LEVENSON: Right.

WAGNER: Where's that letter from Equity, and the what-ever ... stage-hands. *(Tucks it back in his jacket.)* He'll bring up my father, him and my father, *(puts two fingers together)* thirty years ago. "Bobby," he'll say, "Your father was a good man," he'll say, "helped me time and again, your father did." Damn. You'd better do something, you hear that. You'll hand me the check. We'll find out what $51,000 and a lot of B.S. can buy me.

Mayor Wagner must walk a long way to Moses. And as he "enters" and Moses politely rises but does not move away from his chair, cameras flash. At Moses's signal, pate' appetizers are placed before himself and Wagner ...

WAGNER: Commissioner ... ? Your hospital stay, I see, got you back to full strength.

MOSES: *(standing)* You're not sitting.

WAGNER: I never did receive your invitation to this get-together.

MOSES: No? Mr. Seligman? Well. I had no idea. City Hall does complicate the simplest things: you and me, the need for a tete-a-tete. *(Silence)* Bobby. Talk to me. Help me. End this nonsense.

WAGNER: I'll take care of the $51,000.

MOSES: For Park expenses.

WAGNER: Papp will bring the money in person. Accompa-nied by reporters, I'm sure. You'll look damned stupid re-fusing to take it from him.

MOSES: We've re-evaluated. It's not enough.

55

WAGNER: We've done our own evaluation. *(Levenson places down the sheet)* Item by item. It is enough.

Moses glances at it.

MOSES: You've got your father's instincts, a good man, noble man, helped me, time and again, a fine legislator. But you know all that.

Wagner signals Levenson, who places the check on the table.

WAGNER: A check for $51,000. Papp will bring this check to you, $51,000, in person.

MOSES: You are tough, too tough for me.

Moses glances at the check. He motions to Seligman, who picks up the check, hands it back to Levenson.

MOSES: It was enough. Before all this publicity. Now we can expect tens of thousands of people, who think "Julius Caesar" is a salad with croutons.

WAGNER: But they will know a lame excuse when they hear it.

A moment between them.

MOSES: Bobby. *(Gesturing him to sit)* I had him make this pate', you always did like the pate' here.

Moses commences to sit, to eat his. Wagner looks to Levenson, to Moses - still eating - then sits. Moses certainly seems to be concentrating on his pate', until:

MOSES: This is no longer a matter of public funding. This would be public money, money from the Mayor's Office, the Mayor's name attached to it. Which does make a difference. You would not want to contribute money to sponsor a project undermining labor unions. Actors - stage-men - who are not paid union wages - becomes a political matter. *(shrugs)* It's out of my hands. I negotiate with unions, all sorts of unions. Maybe you can convince these unions to make a civic-minded exception.

WAGNER: *(A beat.)* So. That's it. And here I had the impression, according to you this was a simple matter of money.

MOSES: No, I'm not the politician.

WAGNER: What you mean is, you are not elected by the People to your position of power.

MOSES: What I mean is, I'm above the passion and pitfalls of elected office. I'm above you. We both know that. You can't, when the time comes, even refuse to reappoint me. I could drag you through administrative muck and mud for years. We both know that. You see, I'm being honest with you, straightforward.

WAGNER: I can be honest, even a politician like me, can be straightforward. You know, Actors Equity is a small labor union, a small part of the AF-of-L. And the AF-of-L might allow a civic-minded exception in this particular instance.

MOSES: *(shrugs)* "Might". You hope. I know: I have a working relationship with many of those unions.

WAGNER: So do I. The same A-F-of-L whose members, for instance, have just negotiated with me personally a generous contract with their union representing our striking city hospital workers. A few extra medical benefits, a couple words off the record ... *(Hands Moses the letter; now it's Wagner's turn to shrug:)* For Papp, Shakespeare, they're happy to work for peanuts.

Between them, the letter, and a dead silence.

57

WAGNER: *(hungrily indulging in the pate')* The chopped liver here is still OK. What is it? - the egg, the shmaltz, the onion, ...?

MOSES: You are the mayor. I respect that. I did, after all, help you get there. If this Shakespeare thing is more important to you than my continued leadership I will, of course, respect your decision.

Moses signals Seligman, who hands Wagner a sheet of paper. Wagner, still eating pate', reads it.

WAGNER: This is... is this your resignation?

MOSES: I have been cast in the role of the monster. Never before has my judgment been questioned. And in public.

WAGNER: I get asked questions, I get misquoted.

MOSES: A report comes over my desk - I see hundreds every day - a report from my administrator of Central Park, Mr. Constable, Stuart Constable - an experienced man, a trustworthy man - he makes certain recommendations, which seem perfectly reasonable, I initial them, a routine matter. Who could have foreseen ... It's me who gets attacked, I take full responsibility. I wasn't going to throw the man to the wolves - you want me to do that?

WAGNER: Papp gets free Shakespeare, Constable gets a very public lateral transfer. The newspapers have their story, and you have deniability.

MOSES: No. No. It's been made personal, a choice between Mr. Papp and myself.

WAGNER: No, you don't place me in that position.

MOSES: You would not leave it alone.

WAGNER: You've made up your mind. I'll arrange a joint statement ...

A hand on his arm, Wagner's interrupted by ...

LEVENSON: *(to Moses)* You have the press release ready to hand out to the newsmen you've arranged to be waiting outside?

At Moses's signal, Seligman hands over the press release. Wagner starts to read it ...

WAGNER: But this says I demanded you resign over ... issues of park security ...

SELIGMAN: Which is what - in effect - you have done, your Honor.

WAGNER: But you know, you just said, I am in no position to force ...

MOSES: But that is the perception. And that's what counts.

WAGNER: And this list ... *(flipping through page after page of the press release...)* of your accomplishments ...

SELIGMAN: ....Eight single-spaced pages.

MOSES: Well ...

WAGNER: I can't possibly ... I mean, I'll look like, well, a damned ...

LEVENSON: You have an alternative press release, I'm sure.

Once again, at Moses' signal, Seligman is about to hand over the press release to Mayor Wagner, when Levenson intercedes:

LEVENSON: This is on the Mayor's letterhead.

WAGNER: What?!

This just happens to be when Moses signals the removal of what's left of the pate'.

MOSES: A matter of respect. You are the mayor, after all. I'm only a civil servant.

SELIGMAN: A statement of the Mayor's confidence ...

LEVENSON: *(reading it)* "Complete confidence", "grateful for the opportunity to reiterate", "rely on his vast experience", "fully support the Commissioner's decision".

WAGNER: And the list of your accomplishments.

LEVENSON: All eight pages.

MOSES: It's settled then. Tear up this check, and this union deal of yours. The subject of Joseph ...what? - Papp? - is closed. Papp is gone. Before the joint press conference, your Honor...

WAGNER: Press Conference?

MOSES: ... I think we should finish our lunch: the crab cakes with red pepper sauce are excellent.

Levenson intercepts the salad brought in for Wagner, sets it before his own place.

LEVENSON: I think, your Honor, that you should leave Mr. Moses and myself to finish this conversation.

WAGNER: You what? You want me to ... ? What will I tell ...?

LEVENSON: Refer them to me.

WAGNER: And. "My thanks to the Commissioner for arranging his schedule" etc. etc. *(Looks at his watch)* And. Time, I've got time. *(Going to sideboard)* You ever been to a luncheon at the American Canning Institute? I'll take these crab cakes with me. *(Which he does with relish. Then, a finger in Levenson's face)* And. I'm leaving it up to you. You're hanging by the nose hairs, Levenson.

And the Mayor is gone.

LEVENSON: You, Jesse, you should be ashamed of yourself. To be a party to this charade.

SELIGMAN: Sam, I never ... *(looking from Moses to Levenson, as if caught between the two...)* I prepared the one press release ... I never saw the other statement, typed on the Mayor's stationery ... I am sure Mr. Moses will explain his thinking to me ...

LEVENSON: You really think so.

There is no response.

MOSES: *(rising)* I have a busy schedule, Mr. ...

SELIGMAN: ...Levenson.

LEVENSON: This incivility, this ends, here and now. This public spectacle between you and Papp will not continue.

MOSES: Insult me, threaten me - that's your idea of civility? Where were you? Words were spoken here, a scene concluded, between the Honorable Mayor of New York and myself. The matter is closed. Joe Papp is without my support, without the Mayor's support, without the City Council, he is without power. His next step is back into oblivion.

LEVENSON: Don't you understand? Do I have to draw you a picture? The City Council had proposed a tunnel across the Narrows of New York Bay. And then you published drawings of the proposed Verrazano Narrows Bridge, printed by every newspaper in New York. A bridge like that is a beautiful thing. Well Papp has used your own script. Shakespeare under the stars in a public park for a city of people. There is power in beauty like that. That's Joseph Papp's power, the power of public opinion, headline power. It will not end. He won't let this end.

MOSES: Then you'll have to talk to Papp, insult Papp, threaten Papp.

LEVENSON: With what? He's a nothing, a Polack.

MOSES: If the Mayor, or this particular constituency, if they are so concerned about Shakespeare, why don't they fund the park's expenses for this theatre?

LEVENSON: Money is not the problem. You have become the problem. That is the perception. And that's what counts. It was your scenario, many many times, but now it's Papp's. So you know how it will play out.

MOSES: *(turning away)* I'm in recovery. Under doctor's advisement.

LEVENSON: And here I thought we could come to an understanding.

MOSES: Understand this: by tomorrow I'll be in the Bahamas. *(On his way out)* You'll excuse me.

From his folder, Levenson slaps down the sheet of paper:

LEVENSON: Tell me, what these are.

Moses stops, examines it. And remains silent.

LEVENSON: Bonds. Issued to pay for your bridge. The trustees of which are banks run by our people. This one. And this one. *(He points to one after another, down the list.)* There have been delays.

MOSES: There are always delays with large and complex public works projects.

LEVENSON: You'll make me say it? According to the payment schedule set forth in this bond indenture, you are obligated to these banks, these people, to finish so-and-so on such-and-such a date.

MOSES: Technically. The money will be forthcoming. It is, after all, a bridge, a toll bridge. They won't take action, not against me.

LEVENSON: Oh yes they will. This time they will. Breach of covenant, that calls for payment, the full amount of the bond debt, due immediately.

MOSES: In all my forty years, there has never been ...

LEVENSON: There is now. You have the ready money to pay that? *(Silence from Moses.)* And if you can't? - you won't have a bridge, you won't have a Bridge Authority, you won't have bupkes.

Silence, until:

MOSES: You can't bluff a bluffer, Mr. Levenson.

LEVENSON: This is the man's name. He can be reached at this moment at this number *(writing it down),* his private line. Call him. Ask him.

Moses, about to pick up the phone, hesitates. He looks hard at Levenson. Then holds the phone out to Seligman, who seems at that moment like a deer caught in headlights. He takes it, dials the number which, under the gazes of Moses and Levenson, seems to take a long time.

SELIGMAN: Y-yes. I'm calling on behalf of Commissioner Moses, Robert ... He's right here. *(A beat.)* Yes, he has refused to meet your demands. *(A beat.)* You will? *(A beat.)* You will. *(A beat.)* You will.

Silence.
Seligman stares at the receiver for awhile, as if the other side has abruptly hung up.
He finally replaces the receiver.

LEVENSON: So. You'll arrange a meeting with Mr. Papp. Tomorrow.

Moses nods, but only to Seligman.

LEVENSON: You'll do what has to be done to settle this. By tomorrow.

SELIGMAN: *(answering for him)* Yes.

That's not enough for Levenson.

MOSES: Yes.

LEVENSON: Joseph Papp will receive this check for $51,000 from the Mayor. He will be invited to your office. He will then hand his check, for $51,000 - to you. You will accept it, without conditions. Enabling the Shakespeare Theatre to offer free performances in Central Park this summer, and the next, and the next. Am I being clear?

MOSES: To a fault.

SELIGMAN: *(Hands Moses one of the press releases)* Sir? I'm sure Mr. Levenson would agree that, under the circumstances, this press release, stating the Mayor's full support, would be ... acceptable.

Levenson nods his assent. And Robert Moses is gone.

LEVENSON: Thanks.

SELIGMAN: For what? For risking my personal and professional life? Thanks? - for undermining the most powerful man in New York and my own father's hero? Why'd I do that?!

LEVENSON: Because he was wrong.

SELIGMAN: Wrong. He was. He was wrong. And I'm what - young and idealistic?

LEVENSON: A person can be wrong - not evil, ...

SELIGMAN: No.

LEVENSON: Not weak, not stupid, none of that, ...

SELIGMAN: None of that.

LEVENSON: He's none of that - just wrong.

Seligman nods his assent.

SELIGMAN: Whose telephone number was that?

LEVENSON: My laundry service.

SELIGMAN: Oh. No. He's going to check every line of every contract we have with each one of those banks.

LEVENSON: *(he nods)* I'll take care of it.

SELIGMAN: What?! - you mean none of what you told him ...

LEVENSON: I got the idea, I was on my way here, in the limousine, where was the opportunity. Jesse - I have about six hours to call my people, make the necessary arrangements. And then he'll meet with Papp.

SELIGMAN: How do you know?

LEVENSON: You can't bluff a bluffer.

Blackout.

Peggy is standing at the door to their bedroom. Jake scurries in ...

PEGGY: You did not have to come here.

ROSE: He was supposed to get together with me at our office, for the purpose of preparation. So? Nine o'clock, I'm waiting, it's 9:30, no Joe, 9:35, 9:36 ... I'm thinking ...

PEGGY: Don't - alright? - Don't think - Don't worry.

ROSE: No? My God. But this is it - Robert Moses actually invites Joe to a meeting. *(He bangs on the door)* Joe!

PEGGY: Don't you go in there, Jake. He won't come out until he's ready.

ROSE: Right. *(A beat.)* Right. *(A beat.)* Nerves, well sure, panic, but not late, not this, not petrified.

PEGGY: No. Well this is different. This means everything to him.

ROSE: Peggy, he enjoys it - to be on the edge, to drive me crazy. I told him, "Joe," I said, "Keep the day job, Joe."

PEGGY: I telephoned, a Mr. Seligman, I let them know he would be... you know, delayed.

ROSE: Delay?! - Robert Moses?! Our future! A folder in that man's hands! And the folder is now open. And a discussion is about to take place. And Robert Moses - Robert Moses! - is ready to make a deal, I'm sure of it, with us. *(Moves towards front door)* I'll go.

PEGGY: Jake? ...

ROSE: I was not asked - why wasn't I asked?

PEGGY: No.

ROSE: ...I am, after all, a partner in this.

(Voice of) PAPP: The pants ... are wrong!

Dress pants fly out the door.

PEGGY: There. He's alright, he's ready.

(Voice of) PAPP: "This is the day
   That either makes me or fordoes me quite"!

Papp barges through the door, and immediately he's whipping off the tie...

PAPP: The tie's wrong. The jacket's wrong.

Papp is already buttoning the white shirt, he's tucking it into his dungarees ...

ROSE: Don't be crazy. Use your brains not your balls. This is not a cock fight.

PAPP: Jake? - You're wrong.

PEGGY: Jake? - He's right.

ROSE: You will be gracious! You will wear the tie! Wear the goddamn jacket!

PEGGY: *(slipping it back on him)* Wear the damn jacket.

PAPP: His office, I checked it out: it's in a brick building, Roman pillars in front, a wide marble-type staircase.

ROSE: The check! - Where's the check? - $51,000! Where's ...?! *(he finds it in Papp's jacket pocket)* Damn damn damn.   You will hand over this check to Commissioner Robert Moses. He will accept it. It's all arranged. He'll act as if he's being generous, but - listen to me! - he will give in.

PAPP: *(getting Rose's attention)* The newsmen - I want them there.

ROSE: Newsmen?

PAPP: Cameras.

PEGGY: Cameras.

PAPP: Make sure there are cameras.

Chasing after Papp...

ROSE: You don't need to give up free Shakespeare. He knows that, he'll give you that.

Cross-fade to:

The office of Robert Moses .

Moses looks at his watch.

SELIGMAN: It's only six minutes past, sir.

Papp enters. Moses does not stand.
The telephone buzzer sounds. Seligman picks up:

SELIGMAN: No, Mrs. Albright, the guards aren't needed, Mrs. Albright, he's ....Yes, I am sure.

Seligman gestures for Papp to sit in the chair before Moses's desk:

SELIGMAN: We don't have much time.

Papp does not sit. He looks at Moses, as if Seligman is not present.

SELIGMAN: Mr. Papp? - Commissioner Moses. *(No response.)* We appreciate your coming. I think we can arrive at a reasonable agreement here.

A silence.

PAPP: Oh. *(He takes out the check.)* This.

Seligman moves to take the check from him, but Papp does not even acknowledge his existence ... and the check stays in his hand, like a dead fish.

SELIGMAN: Well. To the point. You agree to pay Park Service expenses for the performances we're permitting your theatre. Which we've itemized.

He holds out a few attached sheets of paper.

PAPP: "A tale told by an idiot".

SELIGMAN: Oh. No. I can assure you, other presenters have paid these expenses.

PAPP: No. You're lying.

MOSES: Excuse me?

PAPP: I checked. You made it look like they had paid. This year. For the first time. These presenters made what they called a "security deposit", the source of which was an anonymous donation that was hard to trace. Not hard enough.

Moses signals Seligman, who continues as if nothing had happened:

SELIGMAN: *(on signal from Moses)* Your check, our list of expenses, the agreement. And Commissioner Moses agrees to allow free ...

PAPP: Bob. Thousands of families get out of their hotbox apartments to enrich their lives with a little Shakespeare in Central Park. The people of this city pay for that park, not you. It's their park, not yours. But you wanted them to pay more, not all of them, just those thousands who walk, bus, take the C-train to Shakespeare. You want your pound of flesh.

MOSES: You chose Central Park, fella. Shakespeare could be free for the citizens of this city at Corlears Hook.

PAPP: You know Central Park means something different. Rich people, poor people, theatre people, plumbers, where else but Central Park. You know that - what the hell's the matter with you?

Moses is tight-jawed and rigid. But remains seated.

SELIGMAN: Mr. Papp, I have to ask you ...

PAPP: Sixteen years old, I'm on the fire escape, I remember like yesterday, it is hot, reading the Arden edition of HAM-LET, the words lift me up, over the smell of the garbage and the urine, over the noise of el-trains, of radios, lift me up. I stand there, I have to shout out the lines, they float over the city - I was a kid, a hoodlum, a drop-out - shouting the lines of Shakespeare. It awakened something in my soul. And then, half a lifetime later, on that first night of Shakespeare in Central Park, when 1,000, 2,000, 5,000 people showed up ... I was there again, a kid again. An electric connection, like fate, and I knew right then and there, I knew the meaning of my life. *(A beat.)* You don't understand what I'm talking about - you have no idea.

MOSES: Oh yes. I do.

Between them, silence.

SELIGMAN: *(sensing the mood)* Your check, our list of expenses, the agreement. And Commissioner Moses agrees to allow free admission to all performances, this year and....

Papp places the check before Moses.

PAPP: This year, every year, this buys our freedom, once and for all.

Moses is silent...

SELIGMAN: Sir?

... Moses, looking right at Papp, making his decision.

MOSES: This year.

SELIGMAN: What? - *(taken aback)* But, sir, you can't mean that.

MOSES: This year. Which will give you time to build ...

PAPP: And next year?

Silence: Moses glares at Papp.

MOSES: My statement, the sentence you interrupted, would have been "...give you time to build community support."

PAPP: This buys our freedom, once and for all.

MOSES: Amazing: you make spending other peoples' money an act of social justice.

PAPP: You did that, forty years ago, still do.

MOSES: We build bridges, Mr. Papp. You put on plays.

PAPP: How much will it be next year? A dime? A dime.
Here's a dime for Marcus Evans, Harlem. *(From his
pocket, he slaps a dime on Moses's desk.)* A dime for
Eddie Wong, student.

*He throws this one, hitting Moses. As he does the next ... and
the next ...*

PAPP: A dime for Ben Cohen, retired on Social Security. ...
Tomas Alessandro's dime...

Finally, Moses is on his feet.

MOSES: You lowlife rabble-rousing, presumptuous, ill-
mannered ...

PAPP: This never had anything to do with crowd control, land
erosion. It's about squeezing me dry, forcing me out ...
*(grabs Moses by his collar, both hands, roughly draws him
close)* Gotchya!

Seligman pushes the intercom button:

SELIGMAN: Mrs. Albright! Guards! Somebody! Bring Security!

PAPP: Get your guards, that's right, have me thrown out of
here.

MOSES: Let go of me.

PAPP: Play... your... part.

*Papp holds that moment, eye to eye, until he knows Moses gets
it. Then he lets him go...*

PAPP: *(reverting back to the public spectacle)* I've tried to be
nice, Moses! You stop me and you'll have to carry off
Puerto Rican kids from your back yard and old Jews in

walkers carrying "Save My Shakespeare" signs down 7th Avenue; I'll have actors cursing you at curtain calls after every show on Broadway. *(Being carried out)* No more nice guy, Bob!

NARRATOR: *(as Narrator)* And two park security guards pulled Joe Papp away, carried him by the elbows out the office doors, out the building to the top of its high, wide marble stairway, so much like a stage.

As Moses methodically tears up the check.

MOSES: *(stunned)* Pride and fury, risked everything, damned fool. He did that to me. A man like him. Damn. A man like that.

Cross-fade to Papp: microphones, flashing cameras ...

PAPP: We all respected this man. Some say he's a dictator now, grown old now, out of touch. An intelligent, an honorable, a powerful man, ... He was a hero. *(Shakes his head.)* I'm not an Oxford graduate. All I've got to my name are the .... three dimes and subway token in my pocket. I'm just Joe Papirofsky, a Jew from the streets of Brooklyn. And all I want is for people to have the chance to go over to Central Park on a summer night and enjoy a play by Shakespeare... *(He shrugs.)* Well, you saw what happened. He invites me here, and all he does is call me names, shout down my attempts at reasonable compromise, and have me hauled out of the man's office by his Gestapo.

Blackout.

Dreamscape: Robert Moses, impeccable in his business suit, walks along what seems the endless Verrazano Narrows Bridge.

A steel piece falls loose under his steps. Shocked, he steps up to the bridge railing, which falls off under his hand.

MOSES: What's happening to my bridge?

A steel girder comes flying down past him, crashing into the bay distantly below.

MOSES: What's wrong here? My bridge ...!

Joe Papp saunters into sight, eating a Nathan's hotdog.

MOSES: You. You're dripping mustard - Get off! Get off my bridge! You'll ruin everything.

Papp takes a big bite out of the hot dog and offers it to Moses.

MOSES: I don't like hotdogs. *(Papp stays with him.)* I... *(breaking away)* I never eat hotdogs.

Which Moses now takes, to his own puzzled surprise.
His foot falls through a collapsing walkway. He's stuck.
Papp grabs him by the collars.

PAPP: Gotchya!

MOSES: Don't! We're falling, I'm falling! Let... go....no!.. don't! ...

PAPP: You owe me a dime!

MOSES: That's it? A dime? - that's all this is about?

Steel beams and bolts and cables all tumble past them, splashing into the bay far below.

MOSES: Wake up! Why can't I wake up!

Moses tries to throw away the hot dog...
... But it won't leave his hand.
And Papp let's go, Moses falls, screaming ... in a blaze of light ...

(voice of) MOSES: NOT OVER A HOT DOG!

Blackout.

The elegant, pristine office of Robert Moses. In which Levenson, alone, sits, stands, sits. The large shiny hardwood desk is empty, but for a single thin file folder. Which Levenson hovers over, checking the door, checking his watch. He sits. He stands. He hovers.

Moses, immaculately dressed, enters.

MOSES: Mr. Levenson. Am I late?

LEVENSON: I'm a busy man.

Moses sits at his desk. Without hurrying, he picks up the folder, opens it, reads for a few minutes. While Levenson waits.

MOSES: I've personally read the terms of the bank agreements, checked the dates of our payments.

LEVENSON: And checked, personally, with each and every bank.

MOSES: And I concede, sir. You can put a stop to the Verrazano Bridge, Jamaica Hills Housing Project, all of it. And my lawyers agree.

LEVENSON: And you've read the evening papers - page one, the pictures, headlines, exclamation marks?

MOSES: I have. I realize there is no alternative but to offer *(referring to the folder:)* my letter of resignation.

LEVENSON: This time we'll want to approve that, in advance.

MOSES: I thought you would. Because you wouldn't want the Seligmans' role in this, and the others' to be made public.

LEVENSON: Only a foolhardy person, a naive person, would think to threaten ...

MOSES: A threat? By me? We are talking about long-time business associates, lifelong friends of mine. You know, this Papp fellow's strength is that he's so small-time, and that makes him sympathetic. Unlike bankers. Certain financiers forcing the resignation of a prominent Jewish leader might seem, to the uninformed public, like some sort of ... Mafia. Maybe I'm wrong, tell me I'm wrong, Mr. Levenson.

There is no response from Levenson

MOSES: Yes... Well I also would not want that, not for these long-time business associates, these lifelong friends of mine.

LEVENSON: It would be nothing more than a ... discomfort.

MOSES: To be avoided.

LEVENSON: What do you want?

MOSES: You'll give me time, you and these "friends" of mine. *(A beat.)* I want the Robert Moses name, my name, my reputation. A month. I need...

LEVENSON: Three weeks.

A beat, before Moses nods assent.

MOSES: Enough time for these theatre people to file a lawsuit. An incompetent defense, a handpicked judge... You'll see to it that Papp has the services of a lawyer.

LEVENSON: I'm sure I can find someone.

MOSES: Not yourself of course, a once-or-twice-removed lawyer ...

LEVENSON: Schwartz, Sam Schwartz.

MOSES: The kind of lawyer who might discover a previously unnoticed technicality in the New York Metropolitan Code...

He's at the door...

MOSES: Article 78, Clause 4.

Slow cross-fade ...

The theatre office, messy as ever. Joe Papp, exhausted, lies in his chair, legs on the desk, staring at the ceiling. In the same posture, Jake ROSE, who can't help shaking his head.

ROSE: Joe Joe Joe. *(Silence.)* Did he actually offer you free Shakespeare, on the Great Lawn, in Central Park?

PAPP: He says.

ROSE: No? What? Did you actually - He made the accusation - that you physically grabbed him, you know, by the collar.

PAPP: Grab? Grab him? A man like that? A respected man, an elderly man. Who would believe that?

ROSE: He turned you down, called you names, kicked you out. *(From Papp, a grunt.)* I was at that fur storage day job of mine, thinking to myself "This is the last day I will have to do this cold and stinking job. This is my last day, last hour, last minute in this frigid and odiferous tomb."

PAPP: You underestimate the power of being right, I'm right on this.

ROSE: Uh-huh.

PAPP: I am not beaten. I was called up by HUAC, which was wrong. I wouldn't testify, which was right. Blacklisted, fired by CBS, both morally wrong. And I went to the union, right. Which went to court, right. And I won. "Right" won.

ROSE: My life, finally, could have been full-time in the theatre!

Silence. Papp looks over at ROSE, who is in psychic pain.

PAPP: Jake ... To tell you the truth ... He did offer ... something.

ROSE: Joe? - What are you saying? *(Papp cannot say it.)* He did offer you the Great Lawn, charge a dollar, right, fifty cents, what - And you stood firm ... And he counter-offered ... And ...

PAPP: Offered everything but what's important.

ROSE: And you actually turned him down?!

PAPP: I felt, at the time,...

ROSE: "Felt"? "Felt"?! Joe, use your brain, Joe, it's more than a hatrack!

PAPP: ... It was the right thing, the only thing, to do.

ROSE: You! - You yelled! - you attacked this man! *(grabs Papp by both collars)* You lost it all for us, our last chance!

PAPP: Don't make me hit you, Jake.

ROSE: How could you do this to me?

PAPP: Something will come out of this! I know it - like fact, like fate - I'm certain it will.

Which is just when a lawyer enters.

NARRATOR: When you think "Oh, it's Destiny, it's Fate," most of the time it's just... some lawyer like me. A No-Name lawyer finds overdue bonds in some out-of-the-way account. A lawyer shows up, a lawyer an awful lot like me, Mr. Anonymous, Mr. Nobody, shows up with information about a city code violation. But no. History wants it to be Robert Moses, Joe Papp, like it's a movie, like there are the stars and then there are the bit players. Remembrances and the distance of years and the urge to make everything fit. And here I am, a sidebar, a footnote, me, a minor role.

NARRATOR AS SCHWARTZ: *(referring to ROSE)* You must be Papp.

Looking at his hands on Papp's collar, Rose removes them:

ROSE: No.

SCHWARTZ: *(shaking Papp's hand)* Schwartz, ... Sam. I think I can help you.

PAPP: You've got the testicles of Robert Moses?

SCHWARTZ: I've got a single paragraph from the City Administration Code. About disallowing "arbitrary administrative action."

ROSE: So?

SCHWARTZ: Which might hold up in court. Against Robert Moses.

PAPP: *(A beat.)* I knew it.

ROSE: Who are you?

79

SCHWARTZ: A shirt, tie, the briefcase. I'm a lawyer, consultant, advisor, that sort of thing.

ROSE: A lawyer - means money - We don't have any.

SCHWARTZ: I'd be willing to offer you legal advice pro bono.

PAPP: *(to ROSE)* "Free".

ROSE: Why?

SCHWARTZ: Well. I've been following your story in the newspaper. I hate to see you pushed around by the bureaucracy. Something told me I could help. *(handing over a thick government text)* Article 78, Clause 4, paragraph 3: it can stop Mr. Moses from stopping you.

Rose is reading the paragraph ...

PAPP: Sit down, Mr.

SCHWARTZ: Schwartz.

PAPP: *(to ROSE)* Get Mr. Schwartz a coffee. *(Rose doesn't.)* What do we have to do? - Tell me, anything.

SCHWARTZ: There'll be court papers to file.

PAPP: Cream? Sugar? Jake?

SCHWARTZ: We'll have to do it quickly and get damn lucky - the Superior Court is recessed next week.

ROSE: So, you're saying, he didn't follow proper procedure - look at this, four pages of procedure, it's gobbledegook. I'll bet nobody does this, nobody looks at this, even knows it exists.

SCHWARTZ: It only takes three - you, me, and the judge.

PAPP: You've got a better plan?

He waits; Schwartz waits.

ROSE: We might get the other parks back - the Mayor will try, you heard him, he said that.

PAPP: And we'll go back to some stinking rat-infested concrete wind tunnel on the edge of the East River.

ROSE: What's wrong with that? We belong on the East River, Harlem, Shakespeare belongs at Corlears Hook.

PAPP: Shakespeare won't be sent back into the gutter. Get the man his goddamn coffee! *(Rose doesn't.)* This is theatre - not a new eight-lane traffic jam, theatre - not public housing built like a forty-storey warehouse. Theatre won't be just another public project. Shakespeare won't be some bureaucrat's afterthought.

ROSE: Your pride and my quarter will get us a long ride on the F-train. This is no longer about theatre, about the capital-P-People. It's become about you, about winning. You do this and we lose again, and this time we're locked out of every park, every public building, we're in storefronts, Joe, living rooms, Joe. Goodbye Seventh Avenue, hello New Jersey! I let you fight Robert Moses on the damn dollar deal, and you lost. Let you fight Robert Moses on that anonymous letter of his, and you lost. I let you go into that meeting with Robert Moses himself, and again! again! - you! lost! it!

PAPP: You let me? *(Shakes his head...)* You... let...me? *(...seeing him in a whole different way)* Jake. Jake. It was always between him and me,   always all or nothing, win or die.

SCHWARTZ: I got my own coffee. Gentlemen? I'm sitting down. I am ready to talk.

ROSE: OK, alright, you do what you need to do. Me, I'm temporarily out of optimism. I'm... I'm going to sleep until Tuesday.

With that, Rose turns away, walks out on him.

PAPP: *(turning to Schwartz)* This will work. This will get us what we want. *(To the exiting Jake:)* This is a miracle, that's what! Goddamn deus ex machina!

Cross-fade again, to ...

Robert Moses now sits at his desk, in command, immaculately attired in his formal suit. He's again on the telephone.

MOSES: Julius? Robert Moses. *(A beat.)* She's fine. And ... *(checking his rolodex card)* Selma? *(A beat.)* Your father-in-law, I heard he's recovered completely. *(A beat.)* Tap-dancing lessons? That's wonderful. *(A beat.)* Yes, well, I'll be honest with you, I need a favor. There's a case, concerning the Parks, of no particular importance really, an annoyance really. *(A beat.)* Did I say a word about the issues of the case, one word? This is an inquiry for information, nothing improper. I would not put you in that position.

Moses is smiling ...

Cross-fade to:

Papp's desk is cluttered with papers and folders, which Schwartz is trying to keep organized. Both men are exhausted, Schwartz - his jacket neatly over a chair, tie loosened - showing it in his perseverant meticulousness, Papp - wearing clothes he's slept in - with raw energy, electric, focused.

Schwartz is examining a folder-full of letters:

SCHWARTZ: Am I missing something? This letter of yours follows this letter from the Parks Commission. He formally requests, for the third time he says here, your proposed 1958 budget. And you "look forward", you say here, to his proposed outdoor theatre facility. Proposed.... when?

PAPP: It's not there?

SCHWARTZ: And this: Constable rejects your request to approve and fund three advertisements. You follow immediately with "thanks for your enthusiastic support" and a bill for the three ads in the New York Times.

PAPP: *(grabbing Constable's letter, perusing)* Here it is - can't approve "at this time", he wrote, which was on the 5th. These ads were placed on the 11th. I took him at his word.

This causes an awed, nodding silence from Schwartz.

SCHWARTZ: Ah! His request for the one dollar admission. Here, you agree ...

PAPP: Because I knew, sixth sense, I understood that he would find an excuse to reject that...

SCHWARTZ: Then he wants ...

PAPP: There you are.

SCHWARTZ: ....Two dollars. Then this letter of yours, rejecting the two dollars, the one dollar, the entire change in admissions policy. Which can be interpreted as your request for an appeal. Which - according to City Administrative Code, Article 78 - should have led to a thorough review by Constable, signed off by Moses.

PAPP: *(taking his letter with relish)* Gotchya!

Crossfade to ...

Spotlight on Mayor Wagner, in his limousine, talking on the telephone:

WAGNER: You what?

Another spotlight on Robert Moses, also on the telephone.

WAGNER: Commissioner Moses, let me get this straight: you want an attorney from my office to be defense counsel representing your Parks Commission.

MOSES: I'm only trying to insure the appearance of complete fairness. I think that's important. *(No response.)* Don't you agree?

WAGNER: Fairness, yes, I'm for fairness. You want an attorney from my office ...

MOSES: I trust you'll appoint an attorney who will argue our case vigorously.

WAGNER: An attorney from my office ... I will. Charles Tenney.

MOSES: Tenney?... He's one of your attorneys now?

WAGNER: He's an outstanding ...

MOSES: ... second cousin on your wife's side.

Wagner has no ready response. (He's mumbling something profane under his breath.)

MOSES: Tenney, fine.

WAGNER: Really? Tenney? You're sure?

MOSES: I defer to your judgement, sir.

WAGNER: *(skeptical)* You do. This is ... whose court?

MOSES: Judge Gold.

WAGNER: No.

MOSES: Tomorrow.

WAGNER: Tomorrow?! *(A beat.)* Papp! It's Papp, isn't it?

MOSES: Your Honor, thank you. I knew you'd meet my needs.

WAGNER: ... It's that damn Joe Papp thing!

He hangs up. Wagner is left, completely bewildered.

WAGNER: Damn. *(Into telephone:)* Get me Charles Tenney. Damn. Damn. *(on telephone)* Chuck? Bob. Put that drink down and get over to my office. I have a case for you to lose.

Blackout.

Sound of a judge's gavel.

NARRATOR: At 3 p.m. Friday, June 17th, 1959, Joseph Papp was represented by Samuel Schwartz. The Parks Commission by a member of the mayor's legal staff, who arrived late. At 3:55 Judge Samuel Gold made his ruling:

(Voice of) JUDGE: "No useful purpose is served by the requirement that petitioner make an admission charge. Such a requirement incident to the issuance of a park permit is arbitrary, capricious and unreasonable."

NARRATOR: Robert Moses could have appealed that ruling, he could have delayed, while he "reconsidered" his administrative action. He did neither. At 4:35 Robert Moses made a statement:

MOSES: The court has made its decision. It's not up to me to agree or disagree. All I can do is abide by it. Papp may use methods we don't altogether like, and he may have ideas we don't understand. But, you know, he's a very enterprising fella. All that ever concerned me was his doing permanent damage to park land. So I've recommended to the Mayor that the City itself find the money to fund a permanent theatre facility in Central Park for future Shakespeare performances.

WAGNER: What?! What money? Two- three hundred thousand dollars? From where? I'm only the Mayor!

NARRATOR: The Shakespeare Theatre presented JULIUS CAESAR on the Great Lawn of Central Park, free of any charge, on August 3, 1959.

(Voice of) ACTOR: "According to his virtues, let us use him With all respect and rites of burial."

Joe Papp, as if in the wings, mouths the final words of the performance:

PAPP/THE OTHER ACTOR: "so call the field to rest, and let's away
To divide the glories of this happy day."

Enormous applause washes over him.

Cross-fade as:

NARRATOR: Robert Moses attended groundbreaking for the Verrazano Narrows Bridge ten days later. And then, Robert Moses announced his retirement.

The office of Robert Moses. Which is bare except for cardboard boxes, the model of the Verrazano Narrows Bridge, and the wall of plaques. Seligman is placing the final plaque in place as Moses enters:

SELIGMAN: *(seeing him)* I thought ... you know ... That you would like this, here on the wall, to see before you have to leave.

Moses nods.

SELIGMAN: "American Society of Civil Engineers. Lifetime Achievement".

Moses can't help staring at it.

Meanwhile, at another part of the stage:

Joe Papp is getting used to his new desk - a larger one, on which is his old typewriter and, of course, a telephone. He's banging away on the typewriter, when...

ROSE bursts in:

ROSE: No more cold - stink - no more fur storage! I walked out! For the last time!

Papp continues banging away at his typewriter. This stops ROSE cold.

ROSE: Joe? - Congratulate me? The Shakespeare Theatre's new Associate Producer. *(A beat.)* Don't do this Joe.

Papp continues banging away at his typewriter. ROSE waits. As, at the other part of the stage:

SELIGMAN: It'll be a beautiful bridge, sir.

MOSES: But, you think, at too high a cost: corrupt contractors and unions, displaced neighborhoods.

SELIGMAN: And five years after it's completed it'll be as crowded as a parking lot from 4 p.m. to 7, five days a week.

Silence.

MOSES: Jesse, you'd make a good prosecuting attorney. You'll be OK with Abravanal?

SELIGMAN: It's a fine law firm, sir, thank you.

MOSES: They never lost a case for me.

SELIGMAN: Like Charles Tenney.

A beat.

MOSES: I am sorry it had to be like this, your introduction to public service.

SELIGMAN: It's not what I'd imagined. *(A long beat.)* Sir? I never thought ... this situation in Central Park ... that it would end ....that you would ...

MOSES: You're all guilt and uncertainty. You did something, what, underhanded, something against me. It's alright, Jesse. Don't confess anything. Pretend that I don't know. Don't be afraid. Nobody's afraid of me anymore.

As, at the other part of the stage:

ROSE finally sticks his hand between the roller and the pounding typewriter keys. Papp slams one letter then another then half the keyboard.

Silence.

PAPP: There's no room in the budget.

ROSE: There's the City money, money from the Anspachers, Bernays, Delacorte. I've seen the budget, Joe. There's money in the budget. *(A beat.)* What are you saying, Joe?

PAPP: There's no room in the budget for you.

ROSE: We have an arrangement.

PAPP: We have artistic differences.

ROSE: I did have my doubts. Justifiable doubts. OK, well I was wrong. I admit I was wrong. I stated my opinion - you can't accept a different opinion?

PAPP: It's more than two people with two opinions.

ROSE: You are my friend, we are friends.

PAPP: This isn't personal.

ROSE: We survived the war together. We faced the blacklist together. That makes it personal! We overcame Moses, you and me, together.

PAPP: It was me who beat Robert Moses. I faced him down in public, in court, faced him down eye-to-eye. That's what happened. I was right. You were scared. *(A beat.)* Jake. Listen, Jake ...

ROSE: We'll start over. I'll walk in here, a free man, you'll quote something from "All's Well that ...

PAPP: ... this is how it has to be. This theatre needs a single vision, the right vision, a single voice, my voice, a public personality. That's me, mine, it's my theatre.

Cross-fade to:

NARRATOR: For thirty-five years, Robert Moses had resisted all attempts to allow trucks on the Southern State Parkway to Jones Beach. It would, he declared, ruin its scenic panorama. Within minutes of his retirement, that rule was - at long last - changed. Except, some bureaucrat discovered that every one of its hundreds of overpasses Robert Moses had built... were four inches too low. There are still no trucks on the Southern State Parkway.

Moses has walked to the bridge model, pulls out the one piece of the foundation he had so long ago ...

SELIGMAN: Please! - Sir! - It will ...

...Pulls it all the way out. Nothing happens.

MOSES: It wasn't supposed to happen. The son-of-a-bitch, in ten years he'll be on Broadway.

NARRATOR: It was, actually, eight years.

One might notice, now, Joe Papp hanging a plaque - his first - on the wall behind his new desk.

...Just as Moses - starting at the top left corner - begins slowly, carefully, removing one then another of his wall full of plaques.

Fade-out...

CURTAIN.

**More Great Plays From
Original Works Publishing**

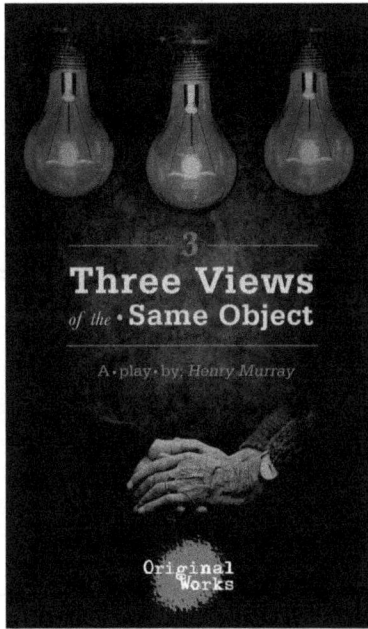

Three Views of the Same Object by Henry Murray

Synopsis: Jesse and Poppy have a suicide pact against the time that illness and infirmity make life impossible to continue unassisted. But what becomes of the pact if one falls ill and the other is still healthy? And how do you know when it's just before being too late? THREE VIEWS OF THE SAME OBJECT offers three different dramatic outcomes to the problems facing the elderly in America.

Cast Size: 2 Males, 2-4 Females

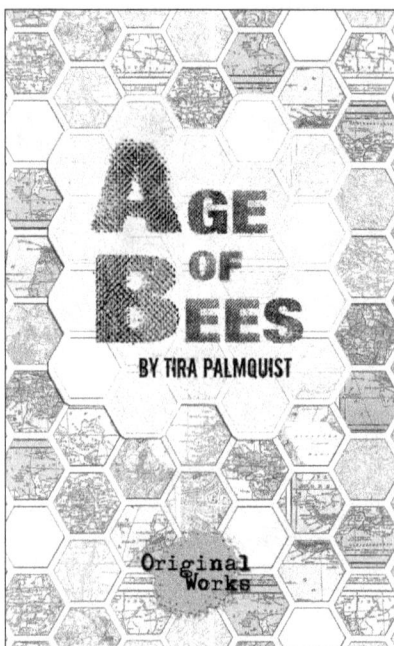

Age of Bees by Tira Palmquist

Synopsis: The bees have gone, disease and scarcity are rampant, but Mel, a young pollinator, finds refuge on an isolated farm. This place is fertile and safe, and Mel counts herself lucky to have a place where – even if it is not exactly happy – she has a purpose. When that purpose and safety are threatened, Mel faces an awful choice: will she risk leaving this relative safety, or will she hide from greater dangers, even if it means giving up some chance that something good can grow in this ruined world?

Cast Size: 1 Male, 3 Females

The Sequence
by Paul Mullin

Synopsis: Renegade researcher Craig Venter develops a controversial "shotgun" technique for sequencing DNA, then quits the National Institute of Health in frustration over an institutional lack of imagination. He quickly makes a fortune in the private sector, and becomes simultaneously the most loved and hated figure of contemporary science. A folksy doctor named Francis Collins inherits the U.S. government's colossal Human Genome Project from no less a giant in the field than James Watson. When his victory in the sequencing race is threatened by Venter, he quickly makes the transition from apparent bumpkin to fierce competitor. Kellie Silverstein, an eager young journalist, cuts her teeth on the biggest science story of all time, the race to decipher the dynamic code of life hidden within the human genome, while she simultaneously runs a race with her own mortality. In the competition to sequence the human genome, will the grand prize be the public good or private profit? And how will three people, amid the frenzied race to determine what makes a human being, discover their humanity?

Cast Size: 2 Males, 1 Female

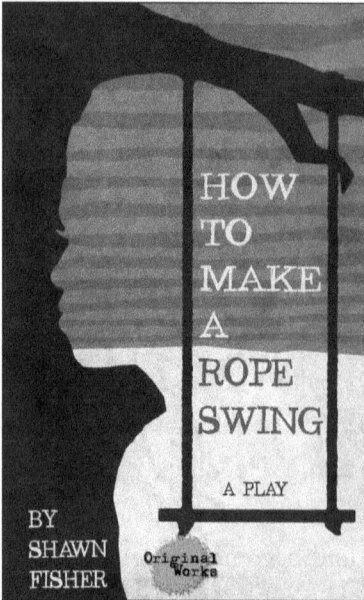

How to Make a
Rope Swing
by Shawn Fisher

Synopsis: Delores Wright is the wealthy town matriarch and former elementary school principal and Bo Wells is the custodian who worked under her strict supervision for most of his life. When they find themselves stranded together in the old condemned schoolhouse, their reunion takes a dark turn and they relive their first meeting, decades earlier. It was 1952, when some schools were first integrated in this region nicknamed the "Mississippi of the North". Bo's wife, the school's first black teacher, was found drowned in a nearby river, hanging by her ankle from an old rope swing after it was rumored she had struck a white child. The papers dismissed it as an accident resulting from the "wild and drunken actions of a young colored woman". When Mrs. Wright reveals that she has dreams about the incident, Bo suspects she knows more than she admits. As the night grows colder and the failing health of Mrs. Wright becomes increasingly evident, Bo tries to understand his wife's final moments and Mrs. Wright's role in her death.

Cast Size: 1 Senior Male, 1 Senior Female, 1 Male (20s)

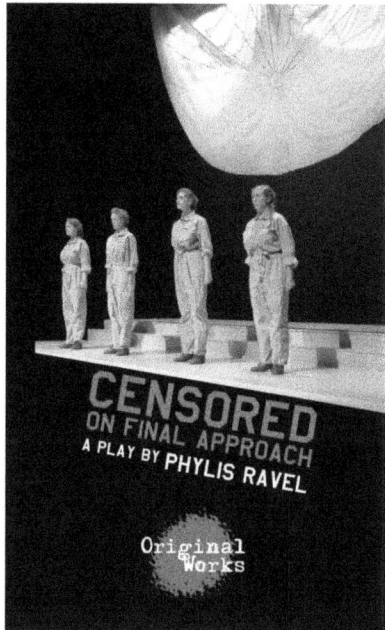

Censored on Final Approach by Phylis Ravel

Synopsis: During World War II a select number of female pilots were selected to serve as WASPs, Women Air Service Pilots. They were not embraced by their male counterparts and struggled for acceptance daily. After the war, four WASPs meet to reminisce about their challenges and successes. The conversation soon shifts to a redacted report about a fellow pilot who was killed while trying to land her aircraft. What really happened? Someone knows the truth. Censored on Final Approach journeys into a time and place often left out of the history books.

Cast Size: 4 Males, 5 Females

NOTES

NOTES

NOTES

NOTES

www.ingramcontent.com/pod-product-compliance
Lightning Source LLC
Chambersburg PA
CBHW062009040426

42447CB00010B/1985